CREATING AN EXCEPTIONAL CULTURE OF
ENGAGEMENT & RESPONSIBILITY

TERRI TUCKER

Copyright © 2020 Terri Tucker

All rights reserved. No part of this book may be used or reproduced by any means, graphic, electronic, or mechanical, including photocopying, recording, taping or by any information storage retrieval system without the written permission of the publisher except in the case of brief quotations embodied in critical articles and reviews.

Because of the dynamic nature of the Internet, any web addresses or links contained in this book may have changed since publication and may no longer be valid. The views expressed in this work are solely those of the author and do not necessarily reflect the views of the publisher, and the publisher hereby disclaims any responsibility for them.

Certain stock imagery © BigStock Images
Any people depicted in stock imagery provided by BigStock are models, and such images are being used for illustrative purposes only.

Prepared for publication by www.40DayPublishing.com

Cover design by Brandi Crane

Additional photography by Joel Baker

Printed in the United States of America

A very special thank you to:

My husband, Les Wiest, who keeps it all in perspective.

Two incredible sons, Connor and Caden Wiest, who teach me something new every day.

My parents.

Dr. James A. Belasco my muse and coach.

David and Colleen Baker, who believe in the power of the game of football and encouraged me to believe.

Phil and Kim Melugin

Mr. Ed Bangs

Coach Lance Gosch

And…The Wolves

Wherever I roam I always ask, "What is the best thing about working here?" No matter what industry, what coast, what continent or what age, the answer always is, "The people I work with." Now I must admit that later in the discussion I ask, "What is the most frustrating thing about working here?" And the answer is always, "The people I work with."

Why?

Teams, businesses, families, each is made up of people. And when two or more are gathered, there is interaction, joy, and frustration. Humans are on a journey of engagement. What are we journeying towards?

>Becoming a part of a PACK!

We are social people. We have the need to PACK! We must belong to something bigger and more important than just the tasks of any given day. We need to matter to someone else or to lots of *someones*.

The journey of the Iron Wolf shines the light on Eight Lessons helping us be better leaders *of packs*. There are healthy *packs* and unhealthy *packs*.

The first place to look for praise or criticism is at The Head Wolf, or the leader of the *pack*.

> If you are leading a team of individuals who need to rise
> above their
> individuality and journey for a larger purpose,
> follow the Eight Lessons.

Character will rise. Goals will come into view. Self-directed action will grow. Ownership and engagement will flourish.

> You will soon have a story worth howling about.

IRON WOLF
Creating an Exceptional Culture of Engagement and Responsibility

In the early morning hours, a rustling begins. A few muffled growls break the silence. Stirring. Anticipation. The Pack is rising for the day. And the click, click, click of the time clock tells us the hunt has begun. It is going to take a great leader to make it a day worth showing up for.

It is not a title that makes the leader of the pack. It is heart and true skill. The greatest of these understand that the lead is never *taken*, it is *earned*.

Eight Lessons of Leadership learned along the journey of the Iron Wolf turn the title into the action.

TABLE OF CONTENTS

PREFACE	11
FOREWORD	17
INTRODUCTION	19
A RISING	21
THE IRON WOLF CHALLENGE	30
THE WOLF AS A MODEL	34
A LITTLE INTERNAL MARKETING	38
LET THE JOURNEY BEGIN	43
THE EIGHT LESSONS OF LEADERSHIP FROM THE IRON WOLF	47
LESSON ONE	49
LESSON TWO	68
LESSON THREE	88
LESSON FOUR	102
LESSON FIVE	115
LESSON SIX	136
LESSON SEVEN	156
LESSON EIGHT	169
THE STATE OF PERPETUAL LEADERSHIP	183
AN AFTERTHOUGHT	186
EPILOGUE	189
SUMMARY OF THE EIGHT LESSONS	191
ABOUT THE AUTHOR	197

PREFACE

Iron Wolf is a story of leadership and learning. It is written through the eyes of a seasoned leadership coach stopped dead in her tracks with the reality of evolving into the mother of a high-school football player.

This book is written in collaboration with an engaged coach at a mid-sized, Midwest high school, his staff of assistant coaches, and a team of young men who strive to make the world a better place.

I am a leadership coach. I am a thought leader. I am a speaker and writer. I am a wife. I am a mother. Always, I am a learner.

Those involved in the creation of this book are not famed leaders. Not one has a title that is recognizable in the Fortune 500 *Who's Who* (except for Dr. James Belasco.) But those that face the hunt every day in the workplace, the home, the community are not famous leaders either. We wake up every day trying to find the path from start to finish and make the journey mean something. The world runs in a progressive direction because good people choose to lead others with their heads and their hearts: doing their best, learning along the way, applying that learning, sharing that learning, and reaping the benefits of high performance.

In *Iron Wolf* I share what I have learned about leadership over my thirty-year plus career in marketing, guest services, experience-creation, facilitation, and consulting. I share stories of leadership success learned in conjunction with my clients. We peek into the best practices of those in the industries of hospitality, health care, education, entertainment, and more. I combine that learning with the first-person discoveries gained by observing a dedicated group of individuals on a football team becoming true champions at life…one teachable moment at a time.

Yes, this is a story about a high school football team in Southwest Missouri. But...the lessons learned are being brought to life in successful organizational cultures throughout our country.

Journey with me as we discover what a leader must do to create teams of individuals who choose to do their very best for a bigger purpose than just a paycheck.

Terri Tucker represents thirty+ years of experience in the arenas of corporate communication, customer experience, and leadership training.

Post-college graduation, Terri embarked on a career as Marketing Director for the Hearst Corporation's KMBC-TV in Kansas City, Missouri. This career position changed course with a move to Springfield, Missouri, as she became Director of Marketing for the NBC affiliate, creating a marketing research and new business development division for Schurz Corporation's KYTV.

In the 1990s, Terri accepted the position of Marketing Manager for Silver Dollar City in Branson, Missouri.

She took with her abilities as an advertising specialist, creative writer, and producer. The corporation identified her internal marketing skills and two years later she was asked to develop and launch a corporate training center built to enhance learning, orient new employees on the company's culture, and annually welcome back the employees who return to work within the seasonal tourism industry of Branson, Missouri.

That invitation was too challenging to pass up and Terri spent six months benchmarking corporate universities and training centers throughout the world. Her entrepreneurial spirit flourished, and she and her team opened Legendary University. In the first year, this unique training center oriented over 2,000 teammates to the corporation's culture. As Director of Legendary University and member of the Herschend Family Entertainment Operating Team, Terri introduced continuing education in the fields of customer satisfaction, salesmanship, and teamwork. One year later, Legendary University opened its doors to external seminars and offered personalized customer service training to hospitality, recreation, and tourism businesses nationwide.

During this time, Terri proudly accepted the coaching and guidance of Dr. James Belasco, author of Teaching the Elephant to Dance and The Flight of the Buffalo. Today, Terri operates her own leadership consulting business, Tucker Resources.

Terri credits most of her success in life to her family. She lives with her two sons and husband, Les Wiest, in Kimberling City, Missouri, on Table Rock Lake…a neighbor to Branson, Missouri.

Coach Lance Gosch knew in high school that he wanted to be a football coach. It was in his blood. His father had built the renowned Webb City Missouri Football Program—13-time Missouri State Champions. He graduated from Pittsburgh State University after a four-year scholarship career and a 62-5-1 record, winning the NCAA Division II National Championship. He began his coaching career at Harrisonville, Missouri, moving to Carl Junction soon after, and then Carthage High School, and Joplin High School. In 1999, he took a huge leap and moved to West Valley High School in Cottonwood, California as Defensive Coordinator. His first head coaching job landed him at Anderson High School in California. Gosch compiled a 27-30 record making the playoffs in four of his five seasons, including winning the Northern Section Division II title game in 2006. Coach Gosch and his wife, Kelli, live near Reeds Spring, Missouri. They have one son coaching football at William Penn University and another son, serving in the Airforce and law enforcement, living in California with their daughter-in-law.

FOREWORD

Dr. James A. Belasco, Best Selling Author, Top Professor, Successful Businessman. When he speaks people listen; when he teaches, people learn; when he coaches, people's lives change to be more successful and meaningful.

Are you searching for a publication that will help you more effectively lead your family, your kids, your small business, or your own personal development and improvement? I am holding in my hand the answer to your quest. The book is:

IRON WOLF
Creating an Exceptional Culture of
Engagement and Responsibility

The author, Terri Tucker, tells her compelling story mixing examples of learning leadership lessons from championship high school football coaches to successful small business owners of real estate offices, mid-sized hotel management firms to rapidly growing medical service organizations.

She then delivers the examples and messages in her own easy to understand language, straight to the point, right from the shoulder, aimed at the heart. I found myself shaking my head up and down several times a page saying to myself, "Go Terri! Bullseye again! Why can't everyone say it so honestly and so beautifully that the reader wants to rush out and *just do it* now!"

When you read the book, I warn you, be prepared for the reading experience—get lots of paper and pencil to make notes on—"things I have to do to be the leader I want to be." I've got 27 pages of single-spaced notes! And, keep a tissue box close at hand. Many of the stories touched my heart and poured the water from my eyes. Terri's book awakened my heart and lit up my brain.

After three reads, I'm convinced that Terri has words of wisdom you haven't heard as clearly and caringly articulated as you will in her book. And, maybe, the applications found in each chapter are the cherries on the top of the hot fudge sundae of the Eight Principles. They are there to tease the reader to seek the greatness of the Wolves—and the hotel Associates—and the Real Estate Agents—and the moms and dads—and any other readers of this book who seek in their lives to "Create an Exceptional Culture of Engagement and Responsibility."

Let's get on with the reading, so we can get on with the doing of the applications.

-*Dr. James Belasco*

Iron Wolf articulates that Greatness in the Game of Football is not just for the Hall of Famer or the NFL player that gets paid for his play. It rests in the important life lessons that are taught every day as a group of boys become a team of men…men who become fathers and leaders in their families, companies and communities that are themselves teams. Terri Tucker tells that story with all the passion of a devoted mother, caring parent, insightful leader and true fan. This is a book for everyone who loves the Game and wants their children (and teams) to have a healthy, happy and productive life of quality & character. Whoever you are and whether you play the Game of Football or not, your ability to lead will be greatly enhanced once you have read this book and made the journey of the Iron Wolf.

-*David Baker,*
President-Pro Football Hall of Fame, Amazing Leader, True Friend.

INTRODUCTION

They walk onto the football field; shoulders are back, uniforms crisp, confidence personified. Each brings his own, but there is more to it. They stand shoulder to shoulder with another in whom they have just as much confidence. They walk hand in hand, but it is more than the physical non-verbal action of holding hands. It is a palpable air of team. They are better together than they are alone. They know it. Everyone who sees them knows it. A unit is entering the arena, not individuals.

It is a team of Iron Wolves. And the team formed—one journey at a time!

It is success.

It is lead—purposefully and intentionally.

It is replicable in any organization.

It begins with the leader and his or her understanding of their real purpose.

All things are possible through great leadership.

A RISING

It was June…summer…time to sleep in, stay in pajamas and drink coffee late into the morning.

"Mom…get up." He shook me gently at first.

"Mom—seriously…get up!" The shaking was more determined. I couldn't ignore it anymore.

"Come on, Connor," I moaned. "There's cereal in the cabinet…help yourself. I just need to sleep a little longer."

"No…I don't want breakfast. You have to drive me to football practice." Connor was serious.

I opened my eyes to see the face of a fourteen-year-old boy—a little excited, a little scared, and totally set on being on time to his first high school summer football weights session.

"I don't want to be late the first day Mom. I've heard stories of what happens when you're late. PLEASE!!!"

And so it began. Four days a week the entire month of June we got up. I got the best end of the deal really. Dad ended up with the take-him-to-practice-at-6:30 am-job, dropping Connor off on his way to work. I grabbed the pick-him-up-at-10:30-job. His enthusiasm and commitment was so inspiring that I actually found myself getting up at 6 o'clock each morning as well and jump-starting the day.

Not once did he give up and just stay in bed. That is remarkable in the world of a 14-year-old who can often times be too tired to take the dog out or pick up his room or put clothes away or mow the grass or carry in the groceries or unload the dishwasher. Not once was he too tired to get up at 6 o'clock and ride twenty minutes to school to lift weights, run, and workout hard for three and a half hours.

I had to learn more about what was happening in this world of football at Reeds Spring High School.

The note came via email:

PARENT MEETING
6 PM TUESDAY IN THE HIGH SCHOOL COMMONS

I had been to Parent Meetings before. They usually consisted of the rules of conduct. Coaches would share their expectations, then politely, but directly explain how they would not discuss play time or other people's children with parents. They would strongly advise parents not to approach a coach on the field directly after a game, but rather schedule appointments to talk. And, invariably there would be a Parent Code of Conduct form. Most Parent Meetings were about corralling the parents so the kids and coaches could do what they needed to do.

After seven years of my husband coaching Mighty Mite Football and Little League Baseball, I totally understood that need.

I was prepared to listen to the speech and sign the be-a-good-parent behavior commitment form.

But something different happened.

It started with an introduction. "I am Coach Lance Gosch. I am the head football coach. I am honored you came tonight. I am honored to serve."

I thought to myself, "Uh huh, *honored to serve*—that is a new twist on coaching."

He took a deep breath and visually scanned across the sea of parents and students. "I look out across this room and I see your sons looking to me and our staff for coaching—coaching to become great football players."

A few parent heads shook in agreement. One man who was jacked on a Monster Energy Drink shouted out an amen-style, "YES SIR!"

The coach smiled but remained resolved to his message. "Reality and history say that very few of these boys, if any, will ever play professional football."

A hush spread across the room as if some truly believed that was a possibility crushed. Monster Energy Drink dude stopped drinking mid sip and offered a challenging stare.

Coach Gosch's volume increased just a bit and his tone deepened. "But I *will* say that over 90% of the boys in this room will become husbands and fathers. Now, I am not naïve. I know my job. We must have a winning record and play some aggressive football. But I am not here to raise professional football players. I am here to help you raise better husbands and fathers...better men. We are going to win some football games; but the ultimate finish line isn't victories on the field.

"We are on a journey that will make lives more purposeful, successful, and rewarding."

And for the second time this summer I was awakened to the power of leadership.

Reeds Spring High School is in Southwest Missouri neighboring the city limits of the tourist mecca of Branson. It is a school district of roughly 2000 kids and 350 faculty and staff. It is a good district with more than 90% of the kids graduating and nearly 60% going on to continue their education in some field. But it is also a district with a high free-and-reduced-lunch population. Money for things like extra-curricular activities isn't easy to find.

The mascot is the Wolf. The Reeds Spring Wolves are a proud pack filled with traditions…good and bad, dating back eight decades. The story that has obtained legend status tells of a time in the community during World War II when families were hungry. The men had gone off to war and the women stayed to raise the children and keep the homes. Like many small communities around our country at that time, families bonded together. Women turned to other women to help them find enough food, harvest crops, and take care of sick kids. The older men helped with repairs and heavy lifting. The community came together—*they packed!* And the mascot for not only the school—but the community was born. The Reeds Spring *Wolves*.

Deep in the fabric stands the core value:

> "We are better together than we are alone!"

The strength of the wolf is in the pack.

The strength of the pack is in the wolf.

The Parent Meeting continued. Coach Gosch introduced his eight-person coaching staff—showing a strong, unified front. Vice Principal of the School and Assistant Coach, Brian Moler stood on one side and, Assistant Coach, Jared Anderson on the other. The respect he held for each member of his staff was obvious. Then he motioned to them to distribute a packet of papers. They blanketed the room like a precision drill team. The first one included Team Policies that defined expectations and rules for engagement:

- → Attendance
- → Un-excused Absences
- → Discipline Procedures—outlined by the State Board of High School Athletics
- → Bus Procedures
- → Grade Average Requirements
- → Drug Testing and Discipline

I thought about all the Human Resources Directors among my client list that must do the same thing every day—handing out packets of rules. "Don't do these things or you will get fired!" I smiled, recalling all the times I have thought we spend more time talking about what *not* to do in business instead of spinning rules into *do these things and you will be successful.*

In my mind, Coach Gosch and his team were beginning to go down the same Rules Highway. I became skeptical.

The next document communicated all schedules with dates and times. Again, linear and formal. But just as he began to explain that document he expanded.

> "Communication is critical in any successful team. And that means communication with all the stakeholders. So, this paper has everything I know about our schedules on it. I have told you everything I know at this time about when and where things are going to happen. No surprises. But things change. I have created a website. I will post changes on that website and communicate to the stakeholder group via that vehicle. Your sons all have a laptop through our school—sit down with your son and have him show you how to access the site and learn about what we are doing throughout the season. We need your help."

I began to think differently about this meeting again. I felt involved and important. The sharing of information through open communication was empowering. This knowledge and accessibility to scheduling empowered each family to be able to plan…plan to be present and prepared. As a busy parent, I valued this transparency very much. I also valued the respect he gave the stakeholder group. Giving us access and encouraging us to work with our sons to obtain that access made my husband and I feel like a part of the team—part of the success equation. A coach that actually used the word *stakeholder*!

I was intrigued.

I was buying in.

The next document distributed was entitled, *Coach-Player-Parent Relations*. I knew this would be the parent-corralling document, but it was truly leadership based versus rule based. In my world of leadership consulting, I would say he was *leading* the parents instead of *managing* us.

> 1. I promise to never embarrass your son, or this school. I ask your son to do the same. We ask you to do the same. I will treat your son just like I treat my own sons. I will love them, and I will always be honest with them. But I will be firm, and my expectations are high.
>
> 2. I am available to talk with you about your son. I will not talk with you about any other player. If you have questions about playing time, ask your son. He should know. If he does not know, have him come talk with me. The answers will not always be what each person wants them to be. But they will get an honest answer. I promise. There are only 22 starters on the offense/defense, so not everyone can be a starter, but everyone has a role on this *team*.
>
> 3. Please do not come to me about a concern right after a practice or a game. That is not a good time for anyone to have a rational conversation. Please schedule a time to talk.
>
> 4. Talk with me. Not my assistant coaches.
>
> 5. Support your son *and* the team. Regardless of the outcome of the season, your son will be a better person for being a part of Wolves Football. Please speak positively about our program in your homes. We cannot be successful if we work against each other.

Once again, we understood the purpose of what we were about to commit to.

We were raising better men.

There was a pause in the agenda. Coach Gosch took a demonstrative breath. I knew something was coming.

> "Our coaching staff, our captains and a few of the leaders on our team have written a Mission Statement."

I couldn't breathe. My heart was flying up to my throat. *A Mission Statement? For a football team?* I was in heaven. I love Mission Statements...the real ones...the ones that are alive in businesses and not simply written to apply for a grant or to be stuck on the wall as art.

My son was going to get the experience of performing underneath the protective and empowering umbrella of a Mission Statement!

And they did it right! They wrote it together as a team!

The Mission Statement read:

> "We will create an atmosphere of Brotherhood, an understanding we are all part of something greater than ourselves. We will establish a culture in which individual sacrifice for the good of the team is the norm. We will build a bond through hard work that will enable us to overcome adversity. We will be accountable to ourselves and our brothers. We will make a choice every day *to be great* in our thoughts and actions. We will develop a relentless attitude towards accomplishing this mission."

As far as eloquent mission statements go, it would not have passed the professionals' filter of concise and catchy, but it was certainly clear. I loved it. It was dripping with passion. It was inspiring and my goose bump meter pegged.

Each stakeholder knew the expectations. And no point in the mission talked about winning football games.

It all addressed the three A's:
Attitude, Atmosphere, and Accountability.

My shoulders pulled back. My chin lifted from the paper.

"My son is on the Wolves Football Team!"

I was so proud and truly freaking out at this moment. As parents, we try to instill character in our home...but to know that he was joining a team lead by character-based men who were going to bring to life the Three A's each day away from home…that is awesome!

We thought he was done, but one more paper was in the packet.

"We have one more defining document which we live by. The Six Pillars. Our Mission rests atop these Pillars. It is what we expect of ourselves as coaches and what we expect of your sons."

WOLVES FOOTBALL

OUR MISSION

We will create an atmosphere of Brotherhood, an understanding we are all part of something greater than ourselves.
We will establish a culture in which individual sacrifice for the good of the team is the norm.
We will build a bond through hard work that will enable us to overcome adversity.
WE WILL be accountable to ourselves and our brothers.
We will make a choice every day TO BE GREAT in our thoughts and actions.
We will develop a relentless attitude towards accomplishing this mission.

OUR MISSION WILL RISE FROM THESE SIX PILLARS

COMMITMENT	CONFIDENCE	COMPOSURE	CHARACTER	ACCOUNTABILITY	LEADERSHIP
All in! The team comes first in all of our actions. Be willing to overcome all obstacles and challenges.	Truly believe in the plan and what can be accomplished. Trust in yourself and your teammates.	Stay focused in all situations. Focus on what we can control and let go of what we cannot.	Do what is right when no one is watching. Understand that all of our actions reflect either positively or negatively on the team.	NO EXCUSES! Give everything you have for your brother next to you. Don't blame outside forces for the outcome.	By example, establish the mission and show others how to achieve it. Motivate and reinforce.

Each of the Core Values of Behavior were spelled out before us like steppingstones to cultural success.

> COMMITMENT: All in, the team comes first in all our actions. Be willing to overcome all obstacles and challenges.
>
> CONFIDENCE: Truly believe in the plan and what can be accomplished. Trust in yourself and your teammates.
>
> COMPOSURE: Stay focused in all situations. Focus on what we can control and let go of what we cannot.
>
> CHARACTER: Do what is right when no one is watching. Understand that all of your actions either reflect positively or negatively on the team.

ACCOUNTABILITY: NO EXCUSES. Give everything you have for your brother next to you. DON'T blame outside forces for the outcome.

LEADERSHIP: By example, establish the Mission and show others how to achieve it. Motivate and Reinforce.

At this point in the Parent Meeting, I was totally satisfied. We understood the purpose of raising young men instead of focusing on producing professional football players. We believed in the goal of accountability. And we bought in.

But then—the most amazing thing happened. I understood, in that moment, why our son was getting up at 6 a.m. every day with passion.

It wasn't about football.

It was about culture.

The culture of a team of Iron Wolves.

THE IRON WOLF CHALLENGE

Everyone assumed the meeting was over. It had been a good meeting—over the line of expectation as far as Parent Meetings go, but Coach Gosch wasn't done. One more document was distributed.

He felt the room ready to wrap. The parents had been conditioned to know that parent meetings were over after the conduct commitment was signed.

> "I'd like to have your attention for just a few more minutes as I present to you our Culture of Excellence. We refer to this as our Iron Wolf Challenge."

The document began:

> "The Wolf is a proud and noble animal. He models the characters of strength, endurance, brotherhood, and intelligence. The Iron Wolf represents the qualities we are looking for in a Reeds Spring High School Football Player. Some of the more premiere qualities are:
>
> → Making Wolves Football a PRIORITY.
> → A driving desire to be GREAT every day.
> → Making the choice to work hard, not for oneself but FOR EACH OTHER.
> → Developing a sense that we are all connected to something BIGGER THAN OURSELVES.
> → Displaying the ability to continually compete at a high level.
>
> These are a few of the characteristics we want WOLVES FOOTBALL to represent."

The leadership coach in me began to do mental cartwheels. I was excited. I knew that having the expectations of attitude spelled out early on in team building is critical. Nothing great can be achieved without a strong culture. Peter Drucker has been quoted saying, "Culture eats strategy for breakfast!" Culture wins in the boardroom, the factory, and the football field. I could see the culture of the Iron Wolf playing out before me. *Commitment, Expectation of Excellence, Purpose, Contribution and Results.* The coaching staff of The Wolves had hit them all with this one document.

Then they proved that it was not just words by attaching the all-important methods of measurement.

> "With these qualities in mind we have set up a point system to help develop an atmosphere of healthy competition within our program and gauge athletes' buy-in to the above expectations. This year—to be considered an 'Iron Wolf' for this Football Season, each player must earn 93% (231) of the possible 248 points available over the course of our summer workout program."

The point system was placed before them. Some of the 248 points could be earned through attendance. Some were achieved by visiting the weight room during the summer while others were awarded for being present at the summer camps. Workout challenges were performance based and could be attained by lifting a certain amount of weight…squatting, curling, and benching. One was based on the speed of a 40-yard sprint.

The next point attainment possibility was truly purpose-driven— remembering that the purpose was to raise better men. Points were available through Community Service…working the Recycling Center, mentoring and coaching Mighty Mite Football, or working the Chain Crew for the little teams' games.

The performance measures were not easy. They were not subjective nor based on who some player's parent was. They were earned. There was only one way to achieve them and that was through hard work and commitment.

I overheard one mother say, "Why on earth would you want to do all this? Is it required to play? I don't want my son working this hard— for what? It's too hard."

The all-important WIIFM (What's In It For Me?) was hanging in the room. *Why* would a player want to do all of this? What is in it for him?

The answer was so very simple and yet so incredible.

> "To add an incentive to this program all designated Iron Wolf Football players will receive an Iron Wolf decal for their helmet…an honor they *earned*. This year's helmet design will change from years past. Everyone will have their number located on the right side of their helmet. Those that qualify for the Iron Wolf will also receive an Iron Wolf emblem for the left side of their helmet. It is our hope that all athletes achieve the status of Iron Wolf. As a team of Iron Wolves, we will be well on our way to meeting the expectations we all have for this Wolves Football Season."

A simple decal to wear on the side of your helmet! Not a $10,000 year-end bonus. Not the status of being fully vested in the 401K. Not even a service watch that tells time. But more motivational than all those combined…to wear the coveted Iron Wolf sticker on the helmet meant "I belong to something bigger than myself." It was an outward statement. "I did it!" And even more importantly, to not have the sticker meant, "I am not there yet."

But the sticker had to be an icon for something truly worth belonging to. Leadership had a challenge ahead of them.

> They had to preserve, promote, and perpetuate
> the regal status of Iron Wolf.
>
> Creating the playing field is not the hard part.
> Development and sustainability are.

The mother in me was thrilled. Our son was nestled within a true *culture*. I have invested over thirty years studying business cultures. Every organization has one. Some are purposeful and guided. Others are happenstance.

> Great leaders don't cross their fingers and hope the culture
> is positive and progressive—they make sure it is.

Great leaders sway the odds in their favor by building a firm foundation: Vision, Mission, Core Values...expectations, codes of engagement.

There are many books highlighting the key ingredients of a successful culture. I have already unveiled the elements that foundationally set up the Wolves Football program to be successful:

- → Vision
- → Mission
- → Core Values/Behavioral Expectations
- → Communication Strategies and Tactics
- → Performance Based Methods of Measurement
- → Reward and Recognition

Iron Wolf is not about the foundational documents, albeit critical. It is about the leader, his or her choices and the behaviors the leader demonstrates that bring those foundational elements to life and CREATE A CULTURE OF EXCELLENCE.

Let us study the behaviors of true champions of leadership.

Let us study WOLF Leadership.

THE WOLF AS A MODEL

A wolf. His eyes shine like a jack-o'-lantern on a pitch-dark night. The wolf is feared and respected all in the same breath. An incredible animal. A skilled hunter. Focused. Protective. Loyal. For centuries, the wolf has been revered as intelligent, instinctive, a spiritual guide, and a worthy opponent.

Behavior proves that the wolf is also a loyal animal, sticking with his or her pack through life and having only monogamous relationships. They are also master communicators, often howling pack prompts across many miles. Non-verbally they convey desire and intent. Body movements, touch, eye contact, and even guttural utterances get their points across. Expression is a strong suit of a wolf.

The wolf is a pathfinder. He does not follow the trails of other animals. He finds his own way and guides his pack in the direction of the greatest success.

The ability to trust is often the most misunderstood trait of the animal due to its frequent nickname *lone wolf*. But the wolf pack is one of the strongest cultural bonds in the animal kingdom. It is very seldom broken, and each member of the pack trusts the other to protect, inspire, emotionally and physically reward, and prosper one another. To be a true wolf is to grant trust and be trustworthy.

I began to realize that Coach Gosch and his team were creating a *pack*. It was intriguing to see the connections. I had to learn more about modeling the behaviors of an actual wolf pack.

One of my clients is the incredible *Boone and Crockett Club*. They are the oldest wildlife conservation organization in North America. Founded in 1887 by Theodore Roosevelt and George Bird Grinnell, this organization initiated and championed America's first National Parks, including Yellowstone, Glacier, Denali, and Grand Canyon. They, too, have a strong culture and solid mission statement:

> "It is the mission of the Boone and Crockett Club to promote the conservation and management of wildlife, especially big game, and its habitat, to preserve and encourage hunting and to maintain the highest ethical standards of fair chase and sportsmanship in North America."

They are also advocates and aggressive marketers of the need to protect and encourage the natural progression of the wolf packs in our country.

I reached out to Tony Schoonen, President of *Boone and Crockett*, to talk about wolves. And he introduced me to a true authority on the matter.

> Ed Bangs was the U.S. Fish and Wildlife Service's Gray Wolf Recovery Coordinator for the Northwestern U.S. from 1988 until his retirement in June 2011. Ed worked his way through college on a cattle ranch, chemical plant, and in the oil fields. He received a B.S. degree in game management from Utah State University in 1974. He received his M.S. in wildlife management from University of Nevada, Reno in 1979. From 1975 until 1988 he worked on a wide variety of wildlife

programs including wolf, lynx, brown and black bear, wolverine, marten, coyote, moose, bald eagle, and trumpeter swan management and research, reintroduction of caribou, and land-use planning and management on the Kenai National Wildlife Refuge in Alaska. Ed was involved with the recovery and management of wolves in Montana, Idaho, and Wyoming beginning in 1988 and led the interagency program to reintroduce wolves to Yellowstone National Park and central Idaho in the mid-1990s. He had opportunities to examine human relationships with wildlife in many other parts of the world, including Mongolia, Africa, Sweden, England, Japan, Italy, and Spain. He published over 120 scientific and popular articles on a wide variety of wildlife management issues. He received the U.S Dept. of Interior *Meritorious Service* and *Distinguished Service* Awards, Special Commendation from U.S. Dept. of Justice, The Wildlife Society Special Achievement Award, Distinguished Alumni of USU, and Awards from the Greater Yellowstone Coalition and Wolf Recovery Foundation.

Wolves, like all highly social animals, depend on the group to make their abilities truly special and valued. Individual wolves are relatively weak (an average male is 100 pounds and average females approximately 80 pounds) compared to fellow creatures like mountain lions, tigers and bears for instance. When a wolf is alone, he tends to stay quiet. Traveling outside of his pack is dangerous. He is vulnerable and nervous about new, unfamiliar stimuli. He loses his curiosity and has difficulty hunting and thriving. The lone wolf spends most of his time either finding a mate to start his own pack or finding a pack to join. He knows his strength is found in a pack. Survivability for a wolf comes from being a part of tight knit team that has a specific task to accomplish.

The pack constantly patrols and defends its territory from strange wolves or neighboring packs so all the resources in it is for that group. They take care of each other. Everyone helps to educate and raise pups. They coordinate attacks on prey to greatly increase their overall efficiency, and attack prey much larger than themselves. Great power comes from that coordination. They share those resources and the rewards which allow a legacy to persist and thrive.

Because of these *rules of the pack* among wolves and their parallels to humans, recent history (the past thousands of years) has allowed wolves and people to have the largest natural distribution of any two land mammals on earth.

A LITTLE INTERNAL MARKETING

The phone rang as I sat in the Parent Pick-Up line at school. Our youngest son, Caden, stood at the doorway of the Reeds Spring Elementary School. At ten years old he was fully decked out in Wolves attire: his hat donned a paw print, he proudly wore his brother's number on his t-shirt, and even his shorts carried the emblem of the enraged and readied Wolf. As I pulled up a little closer, I even saw a cheek tattoo of a bright red paw. It was Friday. Not just any Friday.

FOOTBALL FRIDAY—WOLVES RED DAY!

I answered my cell phone. It was a recorded *All-Call* from Vice Principal and Assistant Coach Brian Moler. It simply stated the time of the home game and the team and mascot we were matching up against. He invited everyone to attend and wear their Wolves Red. The message ended not with a *Goodbye* but a strong and impassioned, GO WOLVES!

> Having an icon to help carry a message is a powerful tool.
> I have seen it work again and again in business to rally a
> team around a message or common goal.

In the '90s I was the Marketing Manager for Herschend Family Entertainment, the largest family-owned themed attractions corporation in the world. Based in Atlanta, Georgia, HFE Corporation employees more than 10,000 associates and offers experiences at 26 locations in 10 states. They own entertainment and themed attraction properties such as Dollywood in Pigeon Forge, Tennessee with partner Dolly Parton; Stone Mountain Park in Georgia; Newport Aquarium in Kentucky as well as the famed Harlem Globetrotters. I was working in Branson, Missouri, at the theme park, Silver Dollar City.

One of my responsibilities was creating and managing the billboards that dotted the landscape on highways feeding the Branson area. There was a moratorium on billboards. They were a precious commodity among the attractions and theatres.

A strong storm blew through the county one autumn and knocked down one of our major boards along the main feeder highway. I knew I had to get it back up and something on it right away before the City would claim it as downed. Maintenance went straight away to fix it and I had the art department print a vinyl wrap as quickly as possible. There was no time to engage the laborious approval process that every board must past through with senior management. I had to do it under the table. I selected a great, smiling picture of one of our street characters hugging a little girl and captioned it, "FRIENDLIEST THEME PARK IN THE WORLD!"

And up the billboard went.

The next day my CEO was driving to work and passed the new sign. Soon my phone rang.

"Hey Terri…did you put that sign up on Highway 65?"

I felt the disapproval in his tone. "Yes, sir…Don't you like it?" Trying everything in my power to persuade with positivity.

"No—not really…But I have a question. Do you believe it's true?"

I was confused. I didn't know what he was asking, so I asked him to repeat the question and he did.

"Do you believe what you put on that board is true?"

I replied, "Friendliest Theme Park In The World?" My voice rose an octave at the end as I was perplexed why he was challenging the words and not the entire board.

He simply answered, "Yes."

I thought for a moment. It was a major turning point in my career and I didn't even know it. I answered how I truly felt. "No—honestly, I think Disney owns that."

And his response was swift and direct. "So, you lied."

It caught me off guard and I reacted the same. I, too, was direct. "No, sir…I didn't lie. I am in Marketing. My job is to entice people to buy tickets. Operations' job is to deliver whatever it is that compelled the people to buy." I was sure I was valid in my response…But I went to school on his words very quickly.

"Young lady—we don't lie. We make promises in Marketing and, as a team, we deliver those promises. So—now that you have put that promise out there into the world of potential guests—you are responsible to make it truth."

My head was spinning. I didn't understand that consequence. Marketing majors in college didn't have to take Ethics courses…just Psych and Persuasion.

"I will give you six months. You figure out how to make us The Friendliest Theme Park In The World. Then come back and begin the process."

Well the rest of the story includes a happy ending. I benchmarked companies all over the world that were known for friendliness. I even spent time in a Goofy costume at Disney. I returned home. And with a creative team of thinkers, we launched *Legendary University*—an Internal Marketing organization that worked to screen friendly people into the company and then train them how to deliver that friendliness in consistent and meaningful ways. We offered front line service training and leadership mentoring. Our mission statement began, "We Create Memories Worth Repeating®." Being friendly was the first step to delivering that mission. Our practices were not Human Resources in nature—they were Marketing. We weren't selling tickets, but we were selling a culture. We were selling our Mission. And our audience was engaging, passionate people who wanted to help touch guests' hearts and facilitate moments in their lives they would never forget. Two years later, Silver Dollar City applied for the *Friendliest Theme Park In The World* award from the International Association of Amusement Parks and Attractions—AND WON!

It was no longer a lie. We delivered our promise.

But the journey of pulling up friendliness and focusing the team on the goal was helped tremendously by the use of an icon. An acorn, to be exact.

The oak tree was a part of the company's history. Jack Herschend, one of the two founding brothers, had always been fanatical about trees, even establishing a corporate construction policy that if one tree was taken down for development, two would be planted in its place. He founded *The Gift of Green Tree Farm* in 1992 with a purpose of re-greening and planting trees throughout Southwest Missouri. It began when the theatre business boomed in Branson and construction was removing many of the trees in the area. He donated trees throughout the area to keep it green. When the EF-5 tornado devastated Joplin, Missouri, *The Gift of Green* sent thousands of trees to rebuild and re-beautify. In its lifetime, *The Gift of Green* has donated over 10,000 trees. The Herschends' theme parks and attractions have always been known and recognized internationally for their beautiful and unique landscaping and mature trees.

Our *Legendary University* team decided the acorn would be an icon for our purpose and support the significance of the oak tree in our company history. Whenever associates graduated from Legendary University, they would be issued a golden acorn lapel pin that was attached to their nametag. It was a symbol of hope, potential, approachability, friendliness, mission success, and team. As soon as it launched it became a coveted item.

If an acorn was lost, my phone rang incessantly until found or replaced. If an acorn was not granted, questions were asked, goals were set, and desire grew. I was amazed. The fifty-cent acorn pin was treasured.

Whenever we had a message to get out to the masses, we posted a bulletin with an acorn at the top of the page. Whenever a recognition was about to happen, we simply placed an acorn sign by the site. The acorn conveyed the message of Mission Driven Behavior...a.k.a. FRIENDLINESS. But most importantly it screamed,

> I am a part of something bigger than myself.

Today, more than a decade later, the acorn is no longer used; but when I visit the park as a guest, I still see them scattered about on the nametags of senior associates. They are a little tarnished and worn but they still make me smile—remembering the power of an icon to drive behavior.

The acorn was an icon with a story to tell.

The wolf is an icon with a story to tell.

GO WOLVES!

LET THE JOURNEY BEGIN

Summer morning merged into summer morning. 6:00 AM seemed earlier and earlier, but my teenager continued to rise. Some days were tougher than others. Tough mornings were quiet. No stories. Head down. Water jug filled without uttering a sound. Easier mornings began with a smile and a nod. But each day's end of practice always resulted the same.

"It was awesome!" was the constant response to the question, "How did it go?"

I smiled after practices each time I heard the energy in our son's tone. I knew the coach was still bringing the culture to life in the summer workouts.

It is so natural to moan when that alarm clock goes off. Our minds race to the things we could do if we didn't have to go into work. We think about lazy summer vacation mornings or the chance to sit and watch a great movie, sip coffee, go for a leisurely walk, stay in our pajamas until noon, shop, spa, clean the house, build something, fix something, golf, cook a great meal, read a book ... But we must get up and go. The difference between great organizational cultures and poor organizational cultures is not in whether the member swears at his alarm clock. Alarm clocks are necessary evil tools. But when we face the devil clock and go to work within a negative or demotivating culture, we return to our beds with the same defeated attitude that hit the snooze button that morning. And the negative cycle of victimizing ourselves to the devil schedule continues.

But when we face that same alarm clock—ever be it with a moan—and we return to set it again with the anticipation of another riveting and inspiringly hopeful day on the upcoming horizon…life is good.

So, even though Connor would never joyfully embrace 6:00 AM in the summer or smile as he downed his breakfast of a spoon of peanut butter and a glass of water, he still knew there was something worth getting up for.

Why?

BECAUSE CULTURE DRIVES BEHAVIOR.

The culture of the Wolves football team is one of *accountability*. You have to be there. You don't want to miss. Every day is important. *Learning* is prevalent. *Challenges* and *rewards* are present. Reputation, respect, and roles are earned in the moments invested together. And, if you are not there—someone else is who is just as eager as you to fill a position and make a difference. If you choose to hit the snooze button and not show up, the peer-to-peer accountability is brutal; plus, you get the joy of running extra on the day you do choose to return.

Consequence is the twin sister to accountability.

Another key point in successful cultures that is often overlooked is—*fun*. Camaraderie is fun. Brotherhood is powerful. You know you are needed on the team for all to be successful. You know you are wanted because of little things—like an upper classman nodding as you delivered a hit; a coach yelling out your name because you did something right; a sense of pride when you looked across the field and mentally say *my* team. One of the biggest indicators is when you find yourself standing up for a brother, a brother who, off the field, is not one of your chosen best friends.

You know you are part of something bigger than yourself.

What you do matters.

The once-in-awhile water fight is fun. The frozen popsicles after a hot practice are fun. Thursday night dinners, breakfasts together on game days, rallies, tailgates…all fun.

As a leadership coach, I have watched many aspiring leaders start cultures. The mission and core values are crafted. The rules of engagement are set. Strategies are identified. Goals are established. Kool-Aid drinkers stand in line and believers rise to the front.

And once the honeymoon is over, the erosion is quick.

One year later the call comes, and we need to rally or review or try to figure out where we went wrong.

> Building a successful culture is not the hard part.
> Sustaining one is.

As the Wolves football team progressed from summer weights to summer practice to fall game season, I watched. The culture sustained.

In fact, it was so strong, it even sustained throughout the school year after the football season ended. It carried over into the next spring and started out full speed ahead three days after the school year ended. I watched the new crop of freshmen parents enter the culture and sit in awe with slightly open mouths at their first parent meeting. And then I watched it again, twelve months later…and again.

> So—what is the secret?
>
> There is none.
>
> It isn't easy. That's why it is rare.

There is no prescribed pill we can take that gives us a positive sustained culture in our workplace, our communities, our schools, our churches, our homes.

It takes hard work, presence, energy, sound foundational principles, a marketing mindset, and a big dose of great leadership.

Why would we want to work so hard?

> Because a positive, empowering, sustained culture can accomplish anything.

It gels life…making both the little stuff and the big stuff worth doing.

> Positivity—Meaning—Purpose—Hope—Fun—Contribution—Accomplishment—Appreciation:
>
> A Life Well Lived.

Coming together and working together for a common, meaningful purpose is natural.

Partnering, pairing up, finding strength in numbers to secure our success is in our nature.

Following the strongest leader and trusting him or her to set a compelling vision has proven to be valid for centuries.

Being social is an attribute of our breed.

Finding a pack in which to truly belong is our quest.

Studying the journey of the Iron Wolf has inspired me to capture eight lessons of building and sustaining a healthy *pack* regardless of the environment in which your *pack* operates. My hope is that my learning will inspire you to apply these leadership best practices to build sustained positive cultures in your circles of influence…whether they be in business, education, family, faith or social settings.

THE EIGHT LESSONS OF LEADERSHIP FROM THE IRON WOLF

It takes Eight to be Great at Leading the Pack.

What is your *Pack*? Each of us find opportunities in life to lead. When a group of people come together because of a job, a cause, a common goal—leaders are needed. Often, there is no roadmap. There is never an *owner's manual* and no two groups of people are the same. But there are some proven best practices to the job called *leader*.

Leadership isn't a science. It is a collection of behaviors. Great leaders choose to deliver specific behaviors that produce results and build strong cultures.

And we begin the journey of discovering eight of them…

LESSON ONE

Cast a Compelling Vision

Wolf Trait

The wolf pack is better together than any one wolf is alone. Legacy persists and thrives. They know their futures depend on the unity shared each day. Within their pack they plan, strategize, and organize to always protect the pack—present and future. There are dens and territories active today that have existed through the generations for hundreds of years…because somewhere, in the beginning, a pack had a vision. And that vision was compelling…telling a story of success, being achieved by being a part of the pack.

It was a simple sentence. He cast it out like a masterful fly fisherman waiting to see if it could tease up a hungry trout. Very few in the room picked up on it. He didn't say it loudly or with flair.

The coach simply said, "I have reserved our rooms in St. Louis for November. It's on my calendar and there is a spot for each of you if you are with us."

The upper classmen knew what he was doing. Smiles cracked across a few faces. A high-five or two surfaced. But very few others even bit.

It was the beginning of the internal marketing of a vision. *November in St. Louis* is Missouri State High School Football Championships.

Now Coach Gosch and his team were not establishing a vision of *winning State*—they had a much bigger idea on the horizon. The vision was one that would change the world. It was lofty, grand, powerful, and real.

BE A PART OF GREATNESS.

It wasn't about *watching* greatness. It wasn't about *talking about* it. It wasn't a vision that had numbers attached to it and it wasn't even truly tangible. But it was *compelling*. It was promising each player that if he signed on and gave it 100%, he would *be* a part of something *great*...True greatness.

To know that feeling and to spend a life questing for it is powerful.

It is terrible to go through life and never be part of something bigger than self...to never know the feeling of having pushed oneself to the point of true challenge and broken through. Greatness isn't an *A* on a report card or a score on a scoreboard. Those are awesome, but they are judged and awarded by another.

> Greatness is an accomplishment—a measurement—
> awarded to oneself by oneself because the heart knows it
> has been achieved. And the heart knows it was difficult.

And when we can learn to self-actualize...to self-motivate in a quest for greatness. We have mastered this journey.

We can ask, "What does greatness look like?" But the better question is, "What does greatness *feel* like?" And once that feeling is achieved—we have to have it. It is like our favorite treat—we crave it.

When being a part of greatness is felt—nothing else will ever do.

So hardcore left-brain readers are about ready to choke at this point. This is not tangible enough! Don't worry. I've got your back.

Casting a compelling vision comes with steps and components, albeit not linear. So…stay with me and the explanation of *how* will come. But challenge your right brain to wake up and embrace the idea of *greatness*. Wear it. Examine it. Understand it. Because it is truly compelling. Knowing what achieving greatness feels like is critical. Because once we feel it, we want everyone we care about to feel it too. And we work to help them achieve it. That is the awakening of the leader. The leader finds fulfillment when he works to create a path for others to journey to greatness.

> If you want to find a great leader, find someone who has played a part in achieving greatness.

I'm going to rock a few relationships with this next statement. I have many friends and colleagues who proclaim a trusted and believed fact at their strategic planning tables and in front of their sales teams:

> "Under promise and over deliver."

I disagree!

Oh, I agree with *plus one delivery*—giving more than the customer expects. It is the most solid repeat-and-refer strategy on the planet. But if your promise is lack luster and not compelling, no one will stick around to find out if you over delivered it or not. No one cares.

In this world of non-differentiated mediocrity, *everybody gets a medal*, the passion suffers. Followers don't run to catch up, they simply crawl along until a bright shiny object catches their attention and they change direction.

But those who cast a compelling vision that is inclusive and promises meaning and purpose—those leaders have a parade of followers running to put their shoes in the right tracks. And even more exciting than that is the vision can lead even when the leader isn't present. One doesn't always have to be setting the path. The vision beckons questers to find a way.

Step One to Casting a Compelling Vision:

Make Sure It Is Truly Differentiating and Compelling... not boring and safe.

The best way to make sure the vision is compelling to others is to make sure others can see themselves in it. We begin by engaging others. We ask them: "What do you think?" "Where should we be headed?" "What is greatness?" "Where do you *want* to go?" "What do you want to be famous for?" "What should our legacy be?"

Coach Gosch asked his leadership team a great question, "What would be a successful season?" Then the leadership team stepped down to the players and asked the same written question.

The coaching staff took all the written answers and began to identify expectations and definitions of *success*. They were engaging in the process of looking through the eyes of those they serve. It is a necessary step in the process of determining the definition of *compelling* and the value of your differentiation.

When the coaches looked through the eyes of those they served, they found passion for a vision—*being great—being part of greatness—pushing, striving, questing for a better team, and better results than they had ever experienced before*. But what they also found was a true desire to craft a Mission.

A Vision Statement is the horizon—the utopian state for which we strive. A Mission is how we are going to get there...what it is going to take...what we do differently and better than the rest of the world we live in. The Wolves believed in that compelling vision—*achieving true greatness as a team while becoming better men*. But they wanted to craft the tangible Mission and follow it with passion.

The answers about what success looked like were compiled. A first draft of a Mission was created. It was shared with the team and discussions flourished about key words and specific meanings. Week after week, multiple meetings were held to discuss *Our Mission*.

Finally, the Mission was complete, and the coaches honored the authors by giving away the credit for its creation.

OUR MISSION: BE GREAT

→ We will create an atmosphere of Brotherhood, an understanding we are all part of something greater than ourselves.

→ We will establish a culture in which individual sacrifice for the good of the team is the norm.

→ We will build a bond through hard work that will enable us to overcome adversity.

→ WE WILL be accountable to ourselves and our brothers.

→ We will make a choice every day TO BE GREAT in our thoughts and actions.

→ We will develop a relentless attitude towards accomplishing this mission.

Step Two to Casting a Compelling Vision:

Look through the eyes of those you serve.
Do not write a vision by yourself for yourself.
It will be a lonely journey.

The compelling vision was created. Now the casting had to begin.

Where most visions and missions break down is not in the writing stage or even the stage that sends the words to the art department and turns them into a pretty document that is worthy of being framed. Where most visions fall short is in identifying the *key behaviors* necessary to bring it into focus.

Meyer Jabara Hotels is one of my dearest and longest-standing clients. They own and operate a diverse portfolio of 23 branded and boutique hotels with more than 4,500 rooms in 11 states. The hotels range in size from 38 rooms to 500 rooms and are operated under licenses from Marriott, Hilton, Sheraton, Holiday Inn, Choice, and Hyatt. The Inner

Harbor of Baltimore features three of the company's most unique boutique offerings, each carrying the exclusive MJ brand: *Harbor Magic*. They have a very compelling Vision and Mission statement that is alive and well within their culture:

Vision

"Empowered associates delivering outstanding hospitality and destination experiences for our guests."

Mission

"To honor, host, and create memorable moments that celebrate life.

"We do this by creating an environment whereby all associates accept empowerment and personal responsibility for: exceptional and distinctive guest experiences, associate development, and profitability."

I remember the first time I stood before a group of new hotel associates and shared this Vision. A young girl about ready to enter the world of housekeeping at a hotel just outside New York City asked me, "What is a *destination experience*?" And on the heels of that question another one fired from an older associate re-entering the workplace after retirement, "I just want someone to tell me what to do—I've never worked in a hotel before. I don't need to be empowered...I need to be trained!"

So—leadership went back to the drawing board. This time we brought with us those two new hires from the orientation class along with a selection of associates throughout the organization that would best represent the 2000+ family.

And the following definitions and explanations were added to the statements:

> Three components are fundamental to achieving the Vision and the Mission of our Company:

Creating a truly engaging Destination Experience in a world where the competition is delivering a basic hotel offering.

Managing a culture which trains dedicated associates to take on the personal responsibility of doing whatever it takes to create a positive, memorable guest experience and then holds each accountable for delivering the same.

Accepting nothing less than a strong foundation of operational excellence…working hard to ensure guest expectations are delivered flawlessly each and every day.

From there we began to:

→ Recruit associates by marketing our Vision and Mission and its definitions.
→ Retain, promote, and continuously train associates who behave congruently with this Vision and Mission.
→ Reward and recognize associates in the moments for delivering the promises made by our Vision and Mission.

Today *Meyer Jabara Hotels* (www.meyerjabarahotels.com) stands at the forefront of hospitality management companies with a vibrant and effective culture.

The mission is the foundation that holds up the culture. And it must be internally marketed.

So…what did the Wolves do with their Mission?

Coach Gosch went back to the words in the Mission and, with a team of leader representatives, began to attach behavioral descriptors to them. The next awesome question was asked,

"What will it take behaviorally for us to get there?
What must we DO?"

Six key words surfaced. And these words became the pillars on which the Mission would stand.

Commitment, Composure, Confidence,
Character, Accountability, Leadership

Next, the great leader did something critically important. He gave the words back to the players. He asked each to write what the word meant to him—individually. He gave them only about a minute or two to write the answer. He didn't want them to overthink it or worry about whether it was in a complete sentence or grammatically correct. He wanted to see heart and true meaning.

He then retreated with papers in hand and pondered the words with his coaching staff.

By the next meeting, the players' words had been fused together into sentences that reflected their hearts and their true desires.

"These are not my words," the coach began. "These are yours. These words were identified by you. Because these words are yours, you must be willing to hold yourselves responsible to them. When you do that—you have the right to hold others accountable to them as well. I am proud of these pillars of character you have created. I am honored to be a part of your team."

And the pillars grew from the roots of the culture:

COMMITMENT

All in. The team comes first in all our actions. Be willing to overcome all obstacles and challenges.

CONFIDENCE

Truly believe in the plan and what can be accomplished. Trust in yourself and your teammates.

COMPOSURE

Stay focused in all situations. Focus on what we can control; let go of what we can't.

CHARACTER

Doing what is right when no one is watching. Understanding that all of our actions either reflect positively or negatively on the team.

ACCOUNTABILITY

NO EXCUSES. Give everything you have for your brother next to you. DON'T blame outside forces for the outcome.

LEADERSHIP

By example, establish the Mission and show others how to achieve it. Motivate and Reinforce.

The Mission statement and the Pillars were graphically enhanced, and a beautiful poster was created. On the first day of fall practice each member of the 72-person team signed the poster. No contract was ever so binding nor so willingly executed. The poster found its home prominently on the locker room wall.

Step Three to Casting a Compelling Vision:

Attach actual behaviors to your vision so everyone knows HOW to get there.

The word *vision* means to picture…to see…to imagine…to bring into view. We must be able to *see it!* The best way to understand the picture associated with a great vision is to wrap it in the palpable comfort of a story.

We are a storytelling culture. Nothing conveys cultural axioms and expectations more than storytelling. For centuries, great leaders have used stories to share knowledge and pass on traditions…to perpetuate culture.

Our culture lives in the stories we tell and within the stories told about us.

If we want our compelling vision to be inculcated into the fabric of our organization, we must wrap it into a story.

Phoenix Home Care and Hospice, based in Springfield, Missouri, is an $90 million company serving the home health needs of patients throughout Missouri and in Kansas, Illinois, and Colorado. The entrepreneurial owners, Phil and Kimberly Melugin, began their organization in 2011 and it quickly grew, receiving top accolades and recognition within the business and health care communities. Their core-values-based style of leadership and focus on mission-driven behaviors caused them to rapidly soar both as a service provider and as a preferred employer. The leadership team consistently brings their mission statement to life through modeling and training the behaviors attached to it.

> "To offer New Beginnings and meaningful opportunities to caregivers and clinicians while providing home care services to our clients built on innovation, skill and Christ-like values of, Patience, Honesty, and Compassion."

Their leadership team spends a lot of time talking about *New Beginnings*. It is at the core of their company values and is born from their actual name. If a client is returning home from the hospital to rehabilitate, they celebrate each day of *New Beginnings* when additional movement or independence is achieved. When a client is fighting depression or lack of motivation, the Caregiver at *Phoenix* will engage in goal setting and vision creation to identify that client's *New Beginning*. And even in Hospice, when this life is ending, the Caregiver talks compassionately with the client about what loose ends he or she regrets and what must be done to ensure each is peaceful about the *New Beginning* awaiting.

The internal marketers at *Phoenix Home Care and Hospice* turned their definition of *New Beginnings* into a story that is marketed both internally and externally:

> *Our Story*
>
> The story of the legend of the phoenix bird is a story of ever-changing growth and rebirth. The beautiful mythical creature reflected the lights and colors of the morning sunrise—always chasing the light and

capturing all that was beautiful. It is a symbol of constant rebirth, renewal and fresh starts. It is not a story of ashes but rather of beauty and upward thinking. (Isaiah 61:3).

Our energy is focused on improving quality of life, perpetuating positive attitudes and embracing the challenges life places before us with grace, respect and compassion.

Our catalyst to consistently rise to new heights is a combination of perpetual learning, measurement of success, looking through the eyes of those we serve and listening with the heart which causes us to pause and discover what is really important in each situation. Within the listening and the application of learning we find *New Beginnings*.

…We are Phoenix Home Care and Hospice.

From this story a culture took flight. Terms like *Believe, Rise Above,* and *Soar* are scattered throughout their website and on the walls of their offices. Their orientation leadership culture course is even entitled, "Taking Flight." The human resource ambassadors who engage with new associates and make sure their first 90 days are indicative of the culture are known as *Flight Attendants*. The reward and recognition program for exceeding client expectations is entitled, *RAFE—Rising Above For Excellence*. The pinnacle leadership award each year is named *The Wing Man Award*.

It is a culture with a compelling vision born from a story about the resiliency and positivity of an iconic image. And the promise for those served rests in the words, *New Beginnings*.

How has this foundation helped a culture grow? The company celebrates nearly ten years of business and incredible growth. Today they stand on stages throughout the Midwest accepting awards that honor Fast Tracking and Economic Impact. Phil Melugin serves as guest speaker, advocating for home care, as our nation strives to better understand and manage the task of caring for the recovering, challenged, ill, and dying.

The *Taking Flight* culture of *Phoenix Home Care and Hospice* is its true differentiator.

The icon of the Phoenix carries with it a message of a quest for greatness.

An icon is powerful. The story of the Wolves vision attached itself to the icon of the wolf. If one would look at the best qualities of a wolf pack in nature—the story of the vision of brotherhood, belonging, self-sacrifice for the good of the whole, protection, determination, overcoming adversity, and a relentless quest for survival would come into full view.

Coach Gosch launched the story of The Wolf Pack and the characteristics of an *Iron Wolf*, wrapping the mission in a once-upon-a-time blanket of marketing. And the mirage turned into a true and possible destination.

Step Four to Casting a Compelling Vision:

Attach a story to your vision.

Tell it often and with passion.

People rise to the vision.

The vision doesn't step down
to be all inclusive and comfortable.

If a deer is present, a hunting wolf pack would never bring back a mouse or a rabbit. Hunting wolves spy their greatest opportunity, balancing success probability with lowest risk and they rise to deliver excellence for their pack. Good enough is never enough.

Everyone on the team (or in the organization) is invited to join the journey to the vision. But those who do not carry their weight are not allowed to travel for long. This is the reality of the wolf pack. If one drags down the pack because of consistent poor performance, lack of effort, or negativity…the pack cuts one and that lone wolf finds a new path to his destination.

Even in social or family settings, the vision should not succumb to mediocrity. *Cutting out* a family member is seldom acceptable in our society—but it is often okay to accept less than excellent, less than our best from each other. Those closest to us—those in our pack—should help hold us accountable and bring out our very best. Why? Because they love us. They know how awesome greatness feels and they want that for us. So—in love, we find accountability. We hold each other accountable because we love each other…because we want the best for each other.

When my training team first began teaching classes at Silver Dollar City's *Legendary University* in Branson, Missouri, we were on fire! The classes were packed with activities, learning, and engagement. We took the mission statement, "We Create Memories Worth Repeating," and dissected it into step-by-step guidelines of how to emotionally link with our guests. We deeply studied the core values, ensuring each Citizen knew how to bring them to life behaviorally. We gelled with a love of serving others and planted seeds of meaning and purpose.

The University was housed inside the home of the original founders of the company, Hugo and Mary Herschend. The walls were decorated with black and white photographs of the early days—when *The Beverly Hillbillies* episodes were shot on grounds; when country music was heard throughout the valleys and when the famed Harold Bell Wright wrote his novel, *Shepherd of the Hills*. A significant framed letter greeted every guest to the University. It was a handwritten note the late Mary Herschend had scribed back in 1955 when the park was a few street performers, an ice cream stand, and beautiful Marvel Cave. It read, "I want this to be as fun of a place to work as it is to visit." I had found the note tucked away in a silverware drawer in her kitchen.

She had cast a vision of fun. After all, it was a theme park. People are supposed to have fun. That is what they pay for. The people in charge of delivering fun should also be having fun. It was a brilliant vision. It was not professionally written, beautifully reproduced, or even grammatically correct. But it was real. It was passionate. It was others-centered. It was compelling.

This *home* facility was the perfect place to welcome new associates into the culture and truly immerse them in the desired utopian state the board, family, and founders had originally dreamed.

We made orientation into the culture fun, in an attempt to begin delivering that vision. Students would ride to the University aboard a school bus. On the ceiling of the bus was a beautiful hand-painted mural depicting the history of the company…beginning with the discovery of the cave and traveling all the way to the present, featuring live performances in the outdoor *Echo Hollow Amphitheater*. A host would teach the history on the path from the park to the University.

Students were greeted on the front porch by University hosts and escorted inside. Once inside, fresh coffee and warm brownies welcomed each. The art of hospitality was demonstrated behaviorally. Then the Mission was shared, and we always included the statement, "We want to welcome each guest into Silver Dollar City as if we were welcoming them into our own homes. The way you feel right now is how we want each of our guests to feel in our parks."

The rest of our day together was spent identifying ways to create welcome feelings, ways to assist, ways to develop heart connections…one guest at a time.

We even covered techniques to recovering guests when something negative happened. The *GUEST* Recovery Program:

G= Give the Guest Respect

U= Understand what the guest is truly saying by empathically listening

E= Explain back to the guest what you hear them saying so you are guaranteed true understanding

S=Solve the problem for the guest—that is our job—figure out what is going to make the guest feel good about their visit

T= Thank them for bringing it to our attention. The only way we can get better is if we know when problems arise. "Thank you for giving us the opportunity to fix it."

For six hours, we touched each new associate and gave them a big dose of the culture. We role played and talked about scenarios. We visited the desires of different demographic and psychographic groups. We discussed how to engage with children—bending down to their eye level. We showed drawings from young child artists depicting adults. The noses of the adults were consistently drawn as two big holes. Why? Because when adults talk to children, they are typically looking down at them. Children look up and see large nose holes. After a good laugh, we demonstrated how to bend down on one knee and talk to the child face-to-face. We shared techniques to demonstrating respect to guests with special needs. Then we would end with a favorite statement, "We cannot make people *feel* important—we simply *make* people important."

Legendary University was thriving. Reviews were outrageously positive. People came to benchmark our training curriculum and asked to sit in on our sessions. Industry leaders sought to buy a seat in our leadership classes.

One day I was asked by a group of park operators to attend a manager's meeting. The meeting was held on grounds in the conference room. I was the last one to arrive. The chairs in the room were set in a crescent shape where six men sat. My chair was staged in the center. Just from the design of the room I knew the *hot seat* was mine.

The first words came from a Human Resources representative. "Share with us what you are teaching at *Legendary University*."

Now each of the men in the room had attended the class already so I knew the question had baggage hanging onto it.

"We are teaching the same stuff we taught when you guys came through the course," I replied.

And then the baggage began to unpack. "Well—(nervousness hung like fog in the room)—we would like you to add a bigger dose of reality to the training."

"What do you mean?" I asked with honest innocence.

And the explanations came. It appeared the operators were frustrated with *Legendary University* because students would leave the courses with a heightened sense of euphoria.

They would believe that their days were going to be positive and happy. Happy guests and happy associates. When they would emerge into the "real culture" there were often crabby associates, angry guests, hot environments and long wait lines. We were not teaching enough reality. The reality was proving to them that we didn't always live up to our mission. Some guests didn't really create memories worth repeating.

I left that meeting without making any commitments to change. The only promise I made was I would review our training and ensure we were talking about realities that face each of us each day.

And that I did. We already talked about crying babies, angry guests, offering mental breaks on hot days along with water breaks, calming down frustration and guest recovery. We even had a dose of conflict management in our curriculum. So, I worried about what the operators were really saying and whether or not our culture was focused on what was positive or on the obstacles that present themselves each day.

Were the realities of working in a labor intensive, guest-centric environment just too much for our associates? Were we not truly leading with the Mission toward the Vision?

What was my role? Teach utopia with a dose of reality or teach mediocrity so as not to set the bar too high to ruffle any feathers? Mediocrity is more comfortable. Mediocrity is easier—no one gets disappointed. But I knew utopia happened at the park—every day. We heard the stories from our guests. We read our reviews. Our season pass sales were the highest percent to attendance in the industry. We were doing right things. So why not teach right things.

I turned to Jack Herschend. He and his brother, Peter, had built this experience. It was his mother who had written the vision of "as fun of a place to work as it was to visit." And he had sat at the table during the creation of the Mission statement. His wisdom was amazing. His heart was altruistic. He would help me.

So—without throwing anyone under the bus, I shared with him my dilemma. I didn't share the story of the operators' challenge. I shared only my own internal angst. "Do I teach so much reality that I lose the dream? Or do I teach the dream and hope reality is not so off course that it clouds the vision?"

In true *Jack style* he answered the question with an amazing question. He looked down at this desk and wiggled a pencil through his fingers. His warm, soft voice remained calm and wise.

> "Terri, if God came to earth today and walked among us do you think He would say, 'Wow—you know, there are a lot of people stealing out there...I think I am only going to have nine commandments. Come to think of it—the prisons are full of murderers...let's just have eight. I know many people out there put other gods before me—so I think seven might be more comfortable for everyone. And I hear about coveting on a daily basis—often coveting the neighbor's wife! So, six is a lot safer...?'"

He paused and just looked at me. Then he made a statement.

> "When you decide what you think God would do about His original vision for the world, you will know your answer."

And so, *Legendary University* continued to teach a utopian vision with a sweetened dash of reality.

> We must have the perfect picture shared with us at some point on our journey or else we will never be able to know if we are progressing toward it.

The compelling vision for the Wolves football team was not to win the State Championship. That is every football team's ultimate vision. It was, and always will be, much bigger than that. Being a part of *greatness* is an achievement that lasts much more than one season or one title. It is also a vision that becomes internalized and carried on beyond the team of the day. It is a life vision. How powerful to be 15, 16, 17 or 18 years old and have a life vision imprinted on your brain!

The vision for the Wolves Football Team was to introduce better men into the world...men of character...men of their word...strong men willing to help up their fellow man. The vision: *Be a Part of Greatness*. Not just watch it. Not just read about it. Not just critique it or even yearn for it. But—be a *part* of it.

WOW! Maybe we *are* raising better men. Maybe we *are* changing the world...one compelling vision at a time.

Step 5 to Casting a Compelling Vision:

Never lower the expectations set by the vision just to make the journey more comfortable for the masses.

The orbit of the earth is caused to happen because of a perfect balance between the motion of the earth and the pull of gravity on it from the sun. The earth would just fly off into infinity if it were not for the sun. The sun keeps pulling the earth and when the sun and the earth play nice together—we stay in orbit. It is a tug-of-war...but it is a good thing. We want this tug-of-war to happen so we all stay alive and prosper.

The *compelling vision* of a team is like the sun to our earth.
It keeps us orbiting and on track.

We must daily acknowledge it—talk about it often—help it rise. It must be ever-present.

APPLICATION

1. Gather a few of your more positive team members together (office staff, family members, organizational members.) Or, you can do it one-on-one. Ask this question, "If you continue to come here every day and work hard, perform your tasks at excellence, and hit your goals, what do you think we are accomplishing together?"

The words associated with their answers do not matter. Compelling visions do not have to be catchy slogans or marketable tag lines. Find out if they truly believe there is a vision for why they do what they do…what we do together. What is our purpose?

2. If you discover that your vision is non-existent or lack luster, begin a quest to write one.

   a. Ask those you serve to help you identify your organization. What do they think about you or your company/product? What benefits do you provide others? What value do you add in this world? What is your brand?

   b. Ask yourself, "What am I passionate about?" "What is important to me?" "What kind of footprints do I want to leave in this chapter of my life?"

   c. Ask your circle, "How do we change the world?"

   d. Then begin to craft the linked words to write a compelling vision.

If you discover that you do have a vision, gather all the answers and hone in on a select group of linked words. Share those words with your circle, giving those who gave input credit for identifying them. Work and re-work the words—getting input several times.

3. Work with your positive vision team to identify what key behaviors—demonstrated daily—are necessary to bring this vision to life. Then define each behavior, challenging yourself, "How will we know we are behaving our way to our vision?" (You may even find your Mission resting in these words.)

4. Begin to package the vision. Once the vision is written and each contributor feels engaged in the final creation, imagine the vision has been achieved and write a story around it. Be creative and dream. Ask yourself, "If this vision came to be—what is a story about life positively impacted?"

Is there an iconic symbol that could help convey our story?

5. Hear yourself telling the story often. Celebrate examples of vision behavior. Live it.

LESSON TWO

Pack

Wolf Trait

Wolves are social animals and they depend on each other to bring out their special abilities. An individual wolf is weak compared to other animals such as lions, bears, or tigers. But when packed together—working together—very few creatures can defeat the pack. They stand together…because of self-preservation…because of cultural code…because it is the wolf way.

Wolves typically do not fight each other within the pack, but they fight viciously against others.

Packs are constantly changing. Wolves come and go based on timing, fate, and abilities. But, like a living organism it adapts and protects to survive. It supports its parts so its parts can support the whole.

The power of the pack is in the wolf. The power of the wolf is in the pack.

Iron sharpens iron.

Proverbs 27:17 says, "As iron sharpens iron so one person sharpens another."

Not a day passes in the Wolves locker room or on the field without the coaching staff talking about playing for the guy next to you.

> "We talk a lot about caring more about the guy next to you than yourself" Coach Gosch shares. "We have to remember there is even a larger group than us that is a part of what we are doing…past players, community, parents. We have a legacy to protect. We need to make sure we are representing them in the right way as well."

Each week during season, a member of the community, a past player, a member of the school administration or a leader from the game of football comes to visit with the Wolves. Coach Gosch secures the speaker. Stories of leadership are shared. Examples of overcoming obstacles are testified. Support is given. At the end of each Thursday night session the individuals on the team share learning realizing even more that what they do matters, what happens matters, how they behave matters…and others are watching. It is a workout for the mind…and the heart.

Former Wolves Offensive and Defensive Lineman, Tanner McMillian, returned from college at Missouri State University to talk with the current Wolves team about what it is like to leave the pack. He spoke of how precious their time is and about the power of the fraternity of football. His passion was electrifying and his rite of passage gave him total credibility. He said, "You will remember—not these days and these games—but these moments. Make each one count not just for you but for your brother!"

After practice one night, Offensive Coordinator, Brian Moler, asked each player to think about the guy next to him on the team. Look around the room and think about each player—identify one for which you are very grateful, think about why you are grateful, and for what are you grateful? Write it down.

The next week they took those moments of gratitude and turned them into a PowerPoint presentation and shared the answers with the team.

The presentation was entitled *Iron Sharpens Iron*. And the posed question was, "From Where Do You Get Your Strength?"

Then the answers flowed:

-from Matt because he blocked for me when I got my first varsity interception

-from Paul who helps me get better by working with me in practice

-from Keenan who reminds me what football is really about

-from Nick who threw me my first touchdown pass

-from Gage—for giving me someone to look up to

-from Dalton for his relentless attitude of brotherhood

-from Jacob who helps me get set on the O Line

-from Tristan who helps me understand the play privately, so I'm not embarrassed

-from Blake D. for starting over me and not only making me humble but making me better

-from Coach Gosch for believing in me and giving me a chance to be a part of it all

-from The Line for sticking together in good and bad times and always having each other's backs

-from John who isn't on Varsity but who still dresses out and comes to every game to support the rest of the team

-from Blake B. for making me practice harder

-from Coach Kess who didn't kill me when I missed my block on the 3rd tech

-from Matt who knocks the piss out of every corner he faces

-from Coach Anderson for pushing me past comfortable

The presentation closed with one slide:

> The Strength of the Pack comes from
> each individual playing for the Pack.

The boys sat pensively. Pride rose in those whose names were mentioned. More pride rose in those whose quotes were selected. As if an unspoken command was heard, each player stood up and took the hand of his teammate. A huddle formed and "Wolves on Three" was shouted. That Friday night The Wolves claimed an outstanding victory.

Coach Lance Gosch knew what it is like to be a part of a pack. He, himself, had been a part of the beginning of a dynasty at a school outside of Joplin, Missouri, Webb City High School.

Today when anyone near the state of Missouri hears the words *Webb City* and *football* in the same sentence, heads turn and ears focus. This football team has forged a path unlike many others. Since 1980 the Webb City Cardinals have not experienced a losing football season. That is over 35 years of expecting to win. And thirteen District 4 State Championships have raised the bar even higher.

When asking Lance Gosch why Webb City has such a successful football program he declares with conviction,

"CULTURE!"

The players, the coaches, the fellow students, the town, the alumni—everyone *expects* the team to win each and every time. They work hard. Everyone supports that hard work. It is a legacy and there is a huge burden of responsibility to carry it forward.

Coach Gosch explains,

> "They have created a wheel of success
> and it is going to be hard to stop it."

In 1964, Tom Gosch, Lance's father, accepted the position of head football coach and kept that role for seventeen years then became Athletic Director for the district and Assistant High School Principal. He created a strong foundation of excellence, character, commitment and mission.

> "My father is a man of great honor and not the type of man you want to let down," Lance shares. "He held all of his boys to a certain standard. And if you did not reach that standard,

he had a way of letting you know that kept you from doing it again."

Coach Lance Gosch paused thoughtfully and smiled.

"He never missed one of my games in high school or college. He was always there. He never talked to me about how I played. It was always about just making sure that I was doing things the right way. If I did my job the right way, then everything else was alright. Each—doing his job the right way!"

That style of leadership imprinted on the hearts of all three Gosch sons. Each boy, born four years apart, enjoyed high-performing football experiences.

Lance Gosch knew post high school that he still wanted to play football. Reality said he would not play the game professionally, but he wanted to stay involved in it as long as possible. Coaching was in his blood.

The Pittsburgh State Gorillas wanted the inside linebacker, Lance Gosch, and brought him in on scholarship. After red-shirting his freshman year he came out aggressively as a Sophomore and graduated in 1993 with a 62-5-1 record. In 1991, they won the NCAA Division II National Championship and repeated to the big game the next year, coming in second.

The combination of a coach father, a winning high school program and a championship college program, lit a fire of questing for greatness inside of Lance Gosch that can only be contained with victories.

He had to have more. So, coaching became his career.

Lance Gosch became Coach Gosch first as an assistant in Harrisonville, Missouri, in 1993. He returned to his own Southwest Missouri at Carl Junction, Carthage and Joplin until 1999 when he took a bold move to California.

The West Valley Eagles in Cottonwood, California love football. During Coach Gosch's reign as Defensive Coordinator, they traveled three times to the championship game and brought home the section title one of those times.

"I was a Junior when Coach Gosch first stepped onto our field," Ross Griffith remembers. "I wasn't sure about him. He was different. He was loud. He was serious." An immerging smile begins to erupt. "I thought to myself, 'Who is this dude? What does he expect from us?'"

It was crystal clear very soon for Ross.

"All Coach Gosch wanted was our very best—all the time. And he wanted us to play for the guy next to us."

"I remember this one time early on in our relationship. I wasn't getting this blocking drill correct. My arms weren't right. He pulled me aside after I did it wrong for what seemed to be the hundredth time and said, 'Ross your arms aren't right. Do it again. You need to do it again.' Oh! I was hot! But I did it."

The smile was still sneaking out of the corner of his mouth as he shared the story.

"Then I actually did it right! Coach Gosch freaked out. He started jumping up and down and yelling. He was so happy for me. *For me* is the point. He was happy *for me*! The really cool thing is he was so loud that all the other coaches noticed me and praised me too. I loved the attention and I wanted to do it right again and again."

Full smile. Pure admiration. Today Ross Griffith is Coach Griffith—at the same West Valley High School in Cottonwood, California. He is the Defensive Coordinator and he loves walking in the footsteps of his mentor.

When Coach Gosch stepped onto the practice field that first year in California he didn't see the biggest defensive players, nor did he see the fastest or the most aggressive. What he saw were hearts and a willingness to learn. It was in 2001 that he first embraced the lessons learned from The Pack. The school mascot was the Eagle not the Wolf…but Coach Gosch used the wolf as an icon to carry his message even in his early days as a coach.

Camp Siskiyou is a beautiful serene spot on the side of Lake Siskiyou at the base of Mount Shasta in Northern California. To have an amazing Defensive Team he had to form a team...a pack. Taking the players from *individual performers* to *team performers* was a process.

The opening statement at camp was never forgotten:

> "You can't be a great football player without being a great citizen. It never happens. Great begets great."

And so, Camp was about learning how to be better citizens—better servants to the guy next to you—better students—better sons—better brothers. In addition to drills and conditioning, the campers heard stories of character and participated in team building activities.

On the last day of Camp, parents and family members drove up to the lake. A grand closing ceremony around a bonfire brought families together. Stories were shared. Successes were honored. And then the moment came that everyone waited for. It was the awarding of the Black Pack Jerseys. Coach Gosch began with the reading of The Pack.

WHY THE PACK?

> In the wild, one lone wolf can't bring down its prey. Its prey will simply outrun it. When that wolf is joined by ten others with the same attitude and goals, its prey has little chance. Those eleven become a pack. If all eleven do their jobs, the pack will eat and grow strong. If just one fails in their assignment, the whole pack could go hungry and grow weak.
>
> The same is true of our defense. It just takes one of us not to do our job and the other team gets a big play or even scores.
>
> We must all develop the same attitude and goals on defense. The attitude will be that NO one will get a yard on us—and if they do, they will pay for every inch of it. The goal is to be the best defense in the Conference—even in the State. If we are all working for these things our defense can only grow stronger.
>
> Commit yourself to working towards these things. Commit yourself to The Pack!

"Starting members of The Pack are..." was the very next line uttered from Coach Gosch's lips. In the still night along the shores of Lake Siskiyou

nothing but a cricket and the crackling fire could be heard. Everyone held their breath as the names were read. It was an *earned* position and a black practice jersey was the outward display of that honor. Each bore the words "THE PACK" on the back.

Wearing the black *Pack* jersey was an honor. There were only eleven of them. But it wasn't a one and done honor. The jersey could be taken away at any time—whenever someone else wanted it badly enough to outperform the guy in front of him. A player could also lose it due to poor grades or lack of discipline. To earn a jersey at camp and keep it all throughout the season meant you were truly contributing to something bigger than just yourself. You were perpetually *earning* your spot on the team.

Coach Griffith carries on the tradition.

> "We still do the Camp and the Black Pack jerseys today. It is still a huge deal. This past year we had an amazing moment. We award black jerseys during Monday Morning Meetings. If someone was being awarded the jersey, we present it on Mondays. This one lineman had been really working hard. He was second string, but he had proven himself over the starting lineman time and time again over the previous two weeks. That starting lineman had started to slack. We decided to award the second-string guy the first-string jersey. When he came to the front of the room he actually broke down and the tears came. I knew he was embarrassed, so we wrapped up the meeting and let him turn back to his seat. When everyone was gone, I walked up to him and asked him why he was so emotional about it.
>
> "He looked up at me and said, 'Coach I have dreamed about this. I have been watching these black jerseys practice since I was in Pop Warner football. My only dream has been to get one. That dream came true today. I am now a real member of The Pack.'"

The power of belonging to something bigger than oneself. WOW— *iron sharpens iron.*

Coach John Kessinger is the Offensive Line Coach for The Wolves. He is tough, skilled, supportive, and encouraging. He will chew a butt with true focus and purpose and then run across the field to hug a lineman that has performed at excellence. His O-Line has been nicknamed *The Wreckin' Crew*. This team-within-a-team labeling has caused the O-Line to truly bond. They stand together. The boys decided to get together and design an icon for *The Wreckin' Crew*. The next step was to order custom t-shirts. In the discussion, each was deciding how much money they could afford per shirt. Money is tight for teenagers. But when the last shirt was ordered, the question rose from the pack, "What about Kess? He needs a shirt." And each chipped in to buy Coach Kess his own iconic shirt. He, after all, was the leader of this mini pack.

🐾 🐾 🐾

Remember the Peter Drucker quote, *"Culture eats strategy for breakfast"*? I have always thought it to be a powerful statement. Leaders can sit around a conference table all day planning and writing goals; but if the people responsible to execute those goals don't buy in and believe their best efforts are necessary to make it happen—it won't happen! They must see themselves at the victory party—benefitting, having fun, and knowing what got them there.

Culture takes a small team of moderately skilled players and carries them all the way to the championship. Culture takes a team of hard-working individuals and turns them into a team of high performers with zero turnover. A culture of accountability and forward thinking equates to positive stratospheric results—not just incremental achievements.

Denise Maiatico is Vice President of *Meyer Jabara Hotels* in the Lehigh Valley. She began her career with the company as Director of Sales for the *Holiday Inn Conference Center* outside of Allentown, Pennsylvania. Her creativity, tenacity and ability to lead were noticed by the owners. When it came time to build a new property in the Bethlehem, Pennsylvania market in 2008, Denise was the obvious choice for General Manager.

Success came quickly and with grand reviews…jumping to the top of the brand's guest satisfaction royalty. One year later she accepted an additional role overseeing yet another property in Bethlehem, *The Hyatt Place* in the historic downtown region. Life was good. Denise and her teams were flourishing. In 2013, Denise was recognized as The

Outstanding Businesswoman of the Year from the Bethlehem Chamber of Commerce.

But just down the road, her original hotel home was floundering. *The Holiday Inn Conference Center* was tired. Having been built in 1988, it looked as though it had seen its grandest days. The movement of commerce and the population of the communities had left it behind. The brand was not hot with the up and coming millennials. Revolving door leadership made stability and mentorship non-existent.

Richard Jabara and William Meyer, owners of *MJ Hotels*, asked Denise to step up. Could she face the challenge of managing three hotels? Could she reinvent the brand of *The Holiday Inn Conference Center* in Allentown? A complete overall and renovation was not in the budget. A few must do upgrades were all that was slated.

Denise accepted the opportunity and her life changed overnight.

I wouldn't say it is easy to lead a fresh team with a bright, shiny new property like *The Courtyard Marriott* and *The Hyatt Place*…but I will say it is a lot easier than to lead a team of people who have not had anything bright, shiny and new in nearly three decades and who have survived by hanging on and riding waves instead of making them.

> Cultures either ride waves or make them.

Denise wanted to join efforts, combine talents and maximize infiltration into the community. Her desire was to create a team of individuals who work together to accomplish amazing results. But the first thing she realized was the three teams had silo mentalities. The two properties in Bethlehem were more unified naturally, but still there was the mindset of *that* property and *my* property. The silo built around *The Holiday Inn Conference Center* was thick and tall! They were not a part of anyone's team.

She also realized that the communities in the Lehigh Valley were *siloing* the three properties as well, not knowing they were all owned by the same company—not aware that the same leadership was at the helm. Denise was a native of The Valley and very much a community activist; yet it was not externally marketed that this parent company was a major player in the hospitality industry and their own local up-and-comer was leading the charge.

Whenever a silo culture exists, it does not allow anything fresh and new to enter the culture, but it also doesn't allow anything to leave. So cultural baggage becomes old, stale, and smelly. Past hurts fester. Past successes become law. Learning stops. The spiral of failure spends swiftly downward.

Silo cultures harbor baggage.

The research began. Denise dove deeply into the real culture of *The Holiday Inn* to discover *the way we do things around here*.

"There are opportunities all around us," she shared with me over coffee. "We just don't see them."

She went on to explain that the culture as she remembered from her Director of Sales days was vibrant and positive. Every stone was overturned. Every chance to serve in the community was embraced. Learning and application were celebrated. Attitudes were positive and grateful. She ached to return to that atmosphere and she also ached to bring along The *Courtyard* and *Hyatt Place* teams to elevate their sense of purpose and ownership of meaningful work.

She quested *great* again.

It was going to take a cultural revival. It was also going to take a revolution. Dr. James Belasco in his book, *Soaring with the Phoenix*, coined this action as a *Revivolution*—renewing the vision, reviving the spirit, and re-creating the success of your company. *Revivolution* is a combination of an old-fashioned revival and a revolution with a dash of revolt! Then the evolution begins.

Denise invited me to help facilitate the journey.

Due diligence required looking through the eyes of the associates and the guests. We needed to shift some paradigms. Our hotel rooms were not filled with beds—but rather opportunities for nights of great, heavenly sleep. Our ballrooms were not filled with tables and centerpieces but instead were stages where life's moments happened: the winning sales pitches, the beautiful first toast as husband and wife, the strategic planning sessions, the birthday party or the unforgettable holiday celebration. Each moment that comes to life within our properties is an opportunity to be a positive memory. So, instead of thinking operationally—we needed to think bigger...more relational.

We needed to bend minds. Whatever we seek we will find. If we seek obstacles we will find them. Likewise, if we seek opportunities, we will find them.

We also needed to shift our attitudes. Instead of finding things that made the days more difficult, we needed to have attitudes of gratitude. We are grateful for every guest that walks in the door and talks with us. We are grateful for opportunities to serve. We are grateful for each other.

We needed more *gratitude* and more *opportunities*. Focusing on gratitude and opportunities gave us a cultural marketing message. We packaged the acronym *GO!*

The GO! LEHIGH VALLEY campaign was born. And the pack began to run.

Denise launched the GO! LEHIGH VALLEY rally cry for not only *The Holiday Inn Conference Center* but also the two Bethlehem hotels. A logo was developed and billboards hit the interstate. Morning stand-ups began to feature stories of Gratitude and Opportunity. We had GO FOR IT! awards and GO! moments. Associates began keeping gratitude journals, and suddenly the conversations began to focus on positive moments and not the drudgery of the days. Each shift began with a sharing of opportunities and ended with a round robin listing of things for which each was grateful.

Today GO! Rallies (stand-ups) happen each morning right out in the lobbies and common areas of all three hotels. It is not surprising to see a guest or two huddle-up and join in the conversation…sharing a personal testimonial of exceptional experiential service.

Denise noticed that the community did not refer to the older property as *The Holiday Inn Conference Center*. It had been a part of the fabric of the Lehigh Valley for so long everyone had a story of a moment which occurred there. The community simply called it *The Center*. She stopped swimming upstream and re-branded to what the people were already saying. The logos were changed, the messaging adapted, and now *The Center* is viewed as the place where memories—past and present—are nurtured and grown. It is the Center of gratitude and opportunity.

The merging of the three cultures into one has helped with expenses as well as associate retention. Job sharing and the gelling of learning happens consistently. Initially, some managers left *The Center* and became *lone wolves*. The *pack* was just too challenging. Change does that.

Ralph left *The Courtyard* in Bethlehem, not because it was too challenging, but because he wanted to further his education. He had been the housekeeping manager. When he finished his education, he wanted to come back but there were no openings at the property and he had to take a job with another company. With the merging of the three properties, he was able to come back to the company at *The Center* as Housekeeping Manager. To say he is excited is an understatement. Culture does that. The once lone wolf came back into the power of the pack and made it better. The satisfaction scores for that department have risen. Ralph challenges each team member each day to do their very best. *Good enough is never good enough.* He is an iron sharpening master!

Today at *The Center* and *The Courtyard* and *Hyatt Place,* it is normal to see an associate bend down and interact with a child, make a teddy bear out of folded towels, or sign a personal birthday card and place it on the bed. We see team members stop to take pictures of guests, offer to carry luggage, open doors, and truly assist. Smiles are abundant. Associates actually like fellow associates and volunteer to help each other.

Recently, the associates produced the Tree of Gratitude where each wrote something for which they were grateful on a paper leaf and stuck it on the tree etched into the glass window. The tree began to reflect life and color. It also reflected how much each associate counted on peers. Many of the leaves bore names of teammates.

From where do you get your strength?

Soon, the guests were talking about the tree and asking if they could take a leaf and add to it. Unbelievable! Who would have thought something so simple would make such a difference? The Law of Attraction flourishes in the Lehigh Valley.

Vibrant, service-centered cultures also produce healthy bottom lines. The first twelve months after the launch of the GO! LEHIGH VALLEY campaign, all three properties were outperforming their competitive sets. *The Courtyard* hit 2.1 REVPAR (Revenue Per Available Room) points over the set. *The Hyatt Place* recorded 7.6

points over and that old, tired *Center* rolled over their competition by a 2.1 point REVPAR growth!

GO! LEHIGH VALLEY! GO DENISE!
GO GREAT LEADERSHIP!

I had the honor of working with C.J. Buck. We were raising money for our Wolves Foundation. C.J. loves children and believes wholeheartedly in education, so he graciously accepted my invitation to speak at our annual *Pack Night at Dolly Parton's Stampede Dinner Attraction*.

Charles "C.J." Buck is Chairman and CEO of Buck Knives, Inc. and the 4th generation to head the family business. C.J.'s grandfather, H.H. (Hoyt) Buck, founded the company in 1902. Hoyt was an apprentice blacksmith, making knives out of files and other workshop scraps. The company grew into a father and son partnership in the forties and was incorporated in 1961 by Hoyt's oldest son and C.J.'s grandfather, Al Buck. C.J. himself started on the production line with Buck Knives in 1978.

Today Buck Knives are shipped all around the world and the name *Buck* is recognized for quality, innovation, and elegant function.

C.J. was inducted into the Cutlery Hall of Fame in 2016, following his father's induction in the '90s and his grandfather's in the '80s.

I first met C.J. while facilitating a board meeting for the *Boone and Crockett Club* at *Bass Pro Shops'* premiere resort, *Big Cedar Lodge*. He's one of only 100 regular members of the *Boone and Crockett Club* and serves on the Club's Board of Directors as Vice President of Communications. He is an avid outdoorsman and hunter, constantly advocating for conservation and ecological balance through the practice of fair chase hunting.

On the car ride from the airport to the Dolly Parton's Stampede Dinner Attraction, we began a discussion about the reintroduction of wolves into the wilderness in Idaho and Montana.

I learned an awesome lesson from C.J. that rings true in business culture as well as in the wolf pack. He explained,

> "You realize…the biggest and baddest wolf in the woods is not the toughest or fastest male. It is actually the one who has mastered social skills!"

I tried to process the thought, not immediately making the connection.

> "The wolf that has learned how to play nice with others and thrive in the pack is much stronger against competitive predators, including hunters, than the lone wolf."

He continued describing *strength*. And I continued to learn. The social wolf lives, not only for himself, but also for the others in the pack. As a part of the pack he is more protected, better fed, better rested, better exercised, and better trained than the wolf on his own.

I smiled when he made the connection back to the football Wolves. "The best team always wins, right?" I nodded in agreement.

> "You can have a couple of rogue studs that think it's all about them; but they can't win championships. If the guy next to him isn't playing for him or even with him, the other team improvises and removes his threat."

The lone wolf costs us wins…he doesn't score wins.

C.J. Buck's company employs more than 300 associates and delivers beyond 2 million knives annually…*as a pack!*

🐾 🐾 🐾

It was still hot outside when I picked up my son from summer practice. The temperature reading in my car registered the outside temperature at 98 degrees. I knew he would be sweaty and smelly when he entered the car.

And I was right.

But this day he popped into the car with a noticeable energy and positive attitude.

I asked, "How did practice go?"

He replied, "Great—really, really great!"

But he didn't share why it was great, he just sat there and smiled. Then he said, as if it was a good thing, "I threw up."

Wow, I thought. So, I had to ask, "And that is why practice was great?"

He explained, "No, Mom!" He had that *seriously-Mom-you've-got-to-get-a-clue* tone in his response. But he was quick to explain what he meant.

> "I am a real part of the team now! We were running sprints. Over and over again we had to run. It was hot. We were in helmets and shoulder pads. Freshmen were dropping like flies. Many were giving up…even some older guys. I didn't give up. I kept going. I threw up a little bit and then got right back in the line. I finished one of the sprints. I thought I was done. I bent down—put my hands on my knees and leaned over. Then it happened…"

I tried to foreshadow—wondering what happened. I couldn't imagine so I just waited until he continued.

> "Josh came over to me. He's a Senior, Mom! He wrapped his fingers into my facemask and pulled my head up. He made me stand straight up. With his fingers still in my grill he said, 'Freshman—We don't go down. We stand up. You want to be a Wolf, you stay up!'"

I looked over at my son. His face was bright with pride. His eyes wide open. I didn't get it. I thought he would be devastated because a first-string starting varsity senior just got onto him. But he wasn't upset at all. He was proud! But I was still confused.

"Are you okay? Was that a *good* thing that he did that?"

He was sort of stunned that I'd asked such an obviously silly question. "Of course, Mom! He wouldn't have taken the time to do that if he didn't think I was worth it. He saw *me!* He said *we* and I was part of that!"

And then I understood the beauty of accountability. At the heart of accountability is the reality of belonging to something bigger than self—belonging to something that truly *needs* your performance and delivery of results. How awesome is that!

> At the heart of accountability is belonging!

Strength and survivability in a wolf come from being part of a tight knit team with each having a specific task to accomplish. All must deliver or be cast out. *Accountability thrives within the pack.* The one that does not deliver on his responsibilities finds himself alone. A lone wolf is a vulnerable wolf.

Once a Wolf Always a Wolf

That is a statement Coach Brian Moler would write at the conclusion of his *Congratulations on Graduation* letter to every Senior football player. The Pack wasn't just about wearing a uniform during high school. It was about learning and working together and becoming a part of something. That didn't go away when someone else wore that number. It became part of a legacy. He would hand a written letter to the graduate player at the end of graduation often writing,

> "I'm very proud and happy to have had the privilege to coach you. That fact that you were a HS football player helps separate you from others. You know what mental toughness is, and the meaning of hard work and family. I believe football is a great game that teaches you things you can't learn other places, and I hope you have learned some lessons to help you along the way. Things like; 1. Anything worth having, you have to work for. 2. In order to be great at anything, you have to pour your heart into it. 3. You can't be afraid to take risks.

> "So many times people fail to accomplish their dreams in life. Most of the time it's because they aren't willing to do what it takes to get the job done, or they allow themselves to get frustrated and give up. If there is one thing I hope playing football has taught you is to Never Give Up. You each have a vision of how you would like your life to turn out. Keep that in your focus at all times, make sure you are working towards that focus every day. People who achieve their dreams do so because they don't allow themselves to get brought down to "good enough" level of the rest of the world. Don't fall into the trap of being negative and/or settling. Make the most of the gifts you have.

> "Once a Wolf, Always a Wolf."

Learning to Pack is a lifelong skill.

Our son, Connor, continued throughout his Freshman and Sophomore seasons with The Wolves, serving on the line playing Varsity and Junior Varsity. Sophomore year his height came. Under the direction of Weightlifting Coach Anderson, his physique began to change. The buzz among parents and some players was that his position should shift…maybe not a right tackle or a lineman. Maybe a tight end or even a receiver. So, one day I just asked, "What position do you want to play?"

He answered with conviction but almost as if it was a silly question. "I want to play football for The Wolves."

I knew the leaders had created a Pack.

Being a part of The Pack is the purpose. Doing whatever each needs to do to create greatness for the pack is the role. The specific position is lower on the significance scale.

Great leaders don't care about title as much as they care about team.

Cultures need to know their *why*. Without a *why* the *how* is simply a job.

APPLICATION

1. Rally. What does it mean to *rally*? It means to *come together* to *reboot,* to *re-energize,* and *reorganize* around something that matters. When was the last time you rallied? Figure out what you want to achieve in the next quarter. Vision it. Identify the behaviors you will need demonstrated by each of your team members and then *rally* around the delivery of those behaviors.

   a. Identify the behaviors
   b. Talk about the behaviors
   c. Attach fun activities to the learning of the behaviors
   d. Incentivize the behaviors
   e. Celebrate the behaviors when you see them happening.

But kick it all off with an old-fashioned pep-rally style meeting.

2. Create a Rally Cry. Pack all the desired behaviors and enthusiasm underneath a Rally Cry that can be internally marketed such as GO! LEHIGH VALLEY—Gratitude and Opportunity.

3. Huddle. Another word for the verb Pack is *Huddle*. Huddle together as often as you can and stand together—talking about the culture. Here is a Huddle rough agenda for a five- to fifteen-minute stand-up meeting:

   a. Welcome everyone to the Huddle.
   b. Share current realities—who you are serving this day; expected numbers; budget goals for the period; general business.
   c. Share any obstacles—turning them into opportunities by asking what we can do about them.

d. Celebrate anything worth celebrating—birthdays, anniversaries, new babies, marriages, etc.
   e. Read your Mission—Why do we do what we do? Purpose!
   f. Rally Cry—share it—discuss it—ask to hear a story about when it came to life. Share a story about the culture working: iron sharpening iron; a great customer comment; a victory or attainment.
   g. Farewell for now.

4. Talk about purpose —being a part of something bigger than just oneself. Talk about team confidence often. Make sure to celebrate team performance more than individual performance. Both are critical but often we spend our reward and recognition efforts on individuals without giving the team contribution a stage.

5. Talk often about how the team efforts influence others. Who does the team serve? How are those lives impacted? Help each find his or her own purpose on the team. Give the team opportunities to look through the eyes of those they serve.

6. Talk about legacy. Does your organization, family, club have one? If so—what is your responsibility to carry it? If not—what do you want it to be? Enable your pack to use it as a vision on the horizon.

7. Ask yourself, "From where do I get my strength?" Take care of your answer.

LESSON THREE

Encourage Tracks

Wolf Trait

"Where have you been?" "What have you done?" "Is there a print of yours left behind or did you simply walk in the paw print of your leader?"

The Alpha Male is the guide not the sole decision maker. His position does not make him the boss; it makes him the influencer. Each wolf has specific skills. The smart Alpha Male knows this and puts wolves in the position where he or she can contribute the most. There is pride in being assigned a task that contributes to the whole.

Wolves are territorial and mark that territory with their scent. Placing their mark communicates ownership. All wolves—not just the boss—mark their boundaries…and tell the story of where they have been.

Did the Captain of the team have influence only after he became the Captain or did the player have influence and become the logical choice for Captain?

Leader is not a title of a position on an organizational chart. If it is in your organization that is a problem.

Leadership is not a title.

Every person on the team should be empowered to lead when he or she is the best to do so.

It was on his ceiling. Each night he stared at it…falling to sleep with it resting on his mind. Each morning he awoke and it was the first thing he saw.

Beat the All-Time Sacks Record

And on the final game of the regular season he did just that. Not only did the dedicated, focused senior linebacker break the all-time sacks record for the season, he also broke it for the most sacks in one game. He broke through the line and found the quarterback for the fourth time in that game. When the whistle blew, he stood and offered his opponent a hand up. The victor was a champion. He had left his tracks.

And, by the way, the whole team won.

One year later the linebacker did the same thing.

Break the Interception Record

And he did. Last game of the season the 8th interception resulted in a pick six.

And by the way, the whole team won.

How does Coach Gosch marry the concept of *team* with the ideal of *individual* record-breaking performance and achieving titles and awards bearing the name of an individual?

Each season ends with individual recognitions. Coach Gosch explains how he feels.

> "I sit and look at a box of awards and trophies that we will distribute at our year end banquet. That box bothers me a bit. I struggle with the individual award and yet I celebrate them too. I love that individual kids are getting recognized for their performance but, in my heart, I know that each member of the team helped each one of these recipients get their awards. I am totally honest when I say that the individual stuff comes because each one bought into the mission and played for the guy next to him. When that happens—we are almost surprised that individually one guy broke a record or received an All-Area award."

> "The individual award is never the goal.
> The individual award is the result."

The Wolves quarterback received the coveted All-Area 3A Quarterback award. It is the most honored award for that position second only to All-State.

I have never heard of an All-State or All-Conference player being selected out of a losing, poor-performing team. The more success a team enjoys; the more individual accolades will surface.

> "That award was earned by our quarterback not because he played for the trophy but because he played every moment of his senior season for the guy standing next to him."
> -Coach Lance Gosch

And then there is the player who played his heart out, aligned perfectly every play and carried out his assignment over-and-over again—never to get singled out for any individual award. Did he leave tracks? Did he make a difference even if the trophies and awards never carried his individual name? Yes! Because he played for the guy next to him. Not for the trophy. And the guy next to him was able to get sacks, grab handoffs, hit holes—and receive trophies. That individual performer must reach inside of himself to find his reward, knowing he served his brothers well.

> The leader encourages individual tracks each day but focuses the individual on the greater good and purpose of those tracks and not on individual recognition.

This Lesson, *Pack*, talks about recognizing and encouraging the power of *team*. But we know that the pack is only as strong as its weakest wolf. Individual performance is key. The leader must encourage each to contribute *at excellence* and leave his own tracks. This answers the questions: What did I do to contribute to the success of the whole? What did I do to play for the guy next to me? This supports accountability through *empowerment*.

The coaches stood shoulder to shoulder against one wall. It was minutes before The Wolves would take the field for the first time of the season. Coach Gosch began the pre-game locker room speech,

> "We are your coaches. We have stood next to you in every practice.
>
> "We have examined every play and watched every placement of every foot and every hand. But now it is time for you to do what you do best. We are not going to be out there on the field with you tonight. When the lights turn on and the game begins, you are going to have to think. You are going to have to act…decide what you should do and find a way to make it happen. It is up to you."

What is empowerment? It is not a buzz word from the '90s. It is a necessary ingredient for success.

> And there are components to building a culture of empowered individuals working together for the success of the whole.

I see many organizations failing at empowerment by encouraging entrepreneurial empowerment—or silo empowerment…asking individuals to perform as if they owned the business. Although it sounds worthy and inspirational, it can create unhealthy internal competition and silos.

A filter that must be added to the empowerment quest is:

> Act as if you own the business and are responsible
> for the success of three key stakeholders:
> customers, associates, owners.

The word picture that supports this is a milking stool. It is a stool with three legs, used throughout the centuries as a dairy stool, to rest on as one milks a cow. Why only three legs? Because, like a tripod, a three-legged stool is always stable no matter what the surface. On uneven surfaces three legs will always touch the ground. Now—if one of the legs is shorter than the others, not true. The stool will fall over.

When we ask someone to make decisions and act, we don't want it to be at the expense of all other stakeholders. We want the business at hand to stay balanced. So, challenge the associate with a question:

> "How is this action going to serve customers, associates and owners?"

In other words, how is the action/decision going to impact the satisfaction and retention or recovery of a customer, the satisfaction and feeling of belonging of the fellow associate(s), the bottom line or fiscal health or brand promise of the organization?

Now, in the football world the question stands, "How is your action going to benefit the success of the team?"

How is it going to support our mission and get us to our vision?

Empowerment is seldom about making decisions when everything is smooth and level. Systems, processes and procedures take care of times of smooth sailing. We need thinkers who take action:

- → When the ground becomes uneven.
- → When things are not going according to plan.
- → When the coach isn't standing right there next to the player.
- → When the customer is angry because of a mishap or poor service.
- → When an associate doesn't show up for his shift.
- → When the play fell apart because an opposing lineman broke through and is seconds away from sacking your quarterback.

It is in uneven times that we need an individual to think and act—to embrace his empowerment…and do what is necessary to create success for the whole.

To do this, there are more key components necessary.

Empowerment sounds like a world without boundaries. Nothing could be more incorrect. For empowerment to truly work there must be:

> a well-defined playing field.

Ever played backyard football? When we were kids, my brother and I always found a pick-up game in our Kansas City suburban neighborhood. Boys and girls joined together for a relatively rough game of *flag* football. My memories tell me, along with the scar on my knee, that it was more tackle than flag. The first thing that would happen would be the marking of the sidelines and the goal lines. Why? Because before we could play we had to know where we could run, in what direction, how far. We needed parameters. There was no game if there was no playing field.

That is also true in leading teams.

When I was researching high performing service-oriented teams during the creation of *Legendary University*, I studied *The Ritz-Carlton*. This amazing hotel company has created systems and processes that encourage ladies and gentlemen to rise to whatever occasion so each can create success for their guests. They have since won the coveted *Malcom Baldrige National Quality Award* twice. I learned during my studies that they had found success empowering their front desk associates by creating a playing field. When a guest was disgruntled, instead of calling for a manager to resolve the issue, the front desk associate was empowered to do whatever he or she thought necessary to satisfy the guest and retain the business. Each associate could refund or reward up to and including $1,999 without a manager's permission.

Now, to me at that point in my career, this seemed ridiculous…putting that much power in the hands of an hourly employee—but it worked for their organization and it worked very well. All the gates stay in check and the employees take that responsibility very seriously. I discovered the reasoning behind the ceiling amount. It defined the expectation. One associate might think refunding a night's stay was too much while another might think it wasn't enough. Some might think giving a voucher for a meal or a drink was spending an exorbitant amount of money while another would consider it an insult. So, by creating a lofty, never utilized amount like $1,999, leadership was saying, "Think! I trust you to think. Do what you think is best to balance the stool and take action. Don't give away the bank—but do what you can do to solve the situation, retain the guest and the business."

When leading the *Legendary University* team for *Herschend Family Entertainment*, we were struggling with a similar situation. The Manager on Duty within the Silver Dollar City team was known as the Park Host. This Park Host was supported by a team of managers known as Division Hosts. There was one top ranking Park Host per day and then a Host for Merchandise, Food, Attractions, Maintenance, and other departments. This team existed to make decisions and act on the spot whenever a system, process, or procedure didn't provide the needed guidance. The number one issue each day was always guest related. A guest might have something negative happen in their experience and seek out a team member to complain. Invariably in those days, the team member would immediately call for the Park Host to solve it.

We needed to change. We knew that the power needed to be put into the hands of the associates to fix it. Guest satisfaction would rise when fewer associates were involved. We wanted the frontline team member to be empowered to take care of the guest situation—balance the stool—make the guest happy and retain the business. We needed to put the power of recovery closest to the guest.

My team created the concept of a *Guest Recovery Voucher*. Each one looked like a check. Every associate was empowered to write something on the tender line that could equate to the cost of a one-day ticket…which in those days was around $50. There was a little push back at first from some other members of leadership. The fear of giving too much away was constricting.

We gave it a trial period.

We deployed a one-hour training session on how to use the tool and guest recovery tactics for each associate.

We internally marketed the successful use of the tool when it happened.

At the end of thirty days our refunds had gone down and our guest satisfaction had risen. Wow! The power of a playing field!

With the one act of creating a well-defined playing field and adding the message of the three-legged stool, permission to think and act was granted.

When we have a team of individual thinkers who take actions for the good of the whole, obstacles shrink. The *find-a-way mentality* is born. Systems and processes don't rule—thinking rules. Individuals *think* about what they need to *do* to find a way to live the mission…make it happen…win!

Two more components to making tracks must be in place to truly have a culture of empowerment.

> There must be training.

The word empowerment includes the word *power*. In this usage, that word has several synonyms: ability; skill; knowledge.

Whenever we define the playing field, we must make sure each individual is the best skilled to run within the boundaries and perform at excellence.

The last necessary component to support a culture of empowerment is critical:

> Acceptance of Making Honest Mistakes
> and Applying Learning

Sometimes along the journey of striving to balance the *stool*, an associate will make a decision and the leader doesn't agree. Although it may be within the playing field and certainly fulfilled the need of the moment, a better decision could have been made.

This is where coaching comes into play. And it is not coaching to *make decisions* the way the leader would make them. It is coaching to make better *balanced* decisions. The leader deploys his role according to this awesome definition I learned from my coach, Dr. James Belasco,

> "Climb on my shoulders and see what you cannot see for yourself."

The coach helps the other person see how their decision impacts the organization. They climb up to a higher viewpoint and see the ripple effect of the decision and then apply the new learning so that next time the decision making is even more balanced.

Dr. James Belasco is my gift from heaven. He landed in my life in the mid-1990s and adopted me as a mentee. I have never looked that gift horse in the mouth. I simply offer humble gratitude for the blessing.

Dr. Belasco led a major computer software and service firm through ten years of phenomenal growth and high margins. He also grew the revenues of a specialty chemical business to the highest margins and market share in its niche. He is the author of the best sellers, *Teaching the Elephant to Dance* and *Flight of the Buffalo*. He is coauthor of the books *Soaring with the Phoenix* and *Seize Tomorrow, Start Today*. As founder of San Diego State University's Management Development Center, with previous tenure at SUNY-Buffalo and Cornell, Dr. Belasco has decades of experience opening doorways to new management structure and reinvention techniques.

I am honored to call him friend.

For me he is the Alpha of my understanding of *empowerment*.

One of the greatest opportunities to see the benefits of true empowerment comes during conflict resolution. In the service industry, there are always moments of angst when a customer expects something to be a certain way and they don't have a positive experience. Weak leaders hold the reigns on this making sure they always get to play hero and save the day. But great leaders let those closest to the customer think about what an appropriate recovery would be and act on that.

Tony Shill is the General Manager of the award-winning, prestigious *New Albany Country Club* in New Albany, Ohio, just outside of Columbus.

Described as the *Gem* of New Albany, Ohio, America's best suburb, (*Business Insider*, October 21, 2015) *New Albany Country Club* is located 12 miles northeast of downtown Columbus in the heart of the New Albany Community. World-class tennis on all three playing surfaces, 27 holes of Jack Nicklaus signature golf, croquet, along with fitness and aquatics offerings, provide 1300 plus members and their families the opportunity to enjoy a wide variety of activities in a resort-style atmosphere.

For 12 years, Tony Shill led the team as General Manager of *Big Cedar Lodge* in Ridgedale, Missouri, the famed rustic elegance experiential resort owned by John L. Morris and the *Bass Pro Shops* family. He accepted the leadership role with New Albany Country Club and headed to Ohio. He has been incredibly successful by casting a compelling vision, *a country club resort where the guest never checks out*. He brought true experiential hospitality to the country club world and led the way to worldwide accolades and prestigious distinction for the entire team.

Tony Shill explains the impact of putting the power into the hands of those closest to the guest.

> "I used to believe that the country club business was like operating a resort without any rooms. Not long after spending time in my new role as GM, I have realized that my initial analogy was incorrect and that it is rather like a resort where the guests never check out.
>
> "In every hospitality business, there are countless moments of truth where the interaction with the customer lasts less than an hour or, at most, a few days. In the country club world, the interaction is forever, and members have exceptionally high expectations. The more we WOW and engage successfully, the higher the expectations rise.
>
> "With this as the backdrop, the opportunity to recover is presented by the hour and in every arena within the business. Employees are expected to know every member's likes and dislikes when it comes to each experience whether it be the use of the health facility, the golf course or one of the food and beverage outlets. I have found it is a true pleasure to build these lasting relationships…very rewarding. But what also

comes with the territory is over the course of the average membership we are privy to behavior that exemplifies both the best and the worst of almost all individuals. That's the way it is with relationships. When a member shares their club with guests, we find the expectations to be heightened and any failure to deliver is very hard to recover.

"I remember a time when we experienced a power outage that left the club and surrounding neighborhoods in the dark at a very critical time—5:30 on a Friday evening. It was the weekend before Christmas and we had planned for a large group of member children to sing carols in the Living Room. This is a cherished club tradition always followed by the families involved enjoying dinner in the Family Dining Room. We also had a full reservation sheet and without knowing how long the power would be out we all went into Plan B mode preparing to offer a buffet to the 150 or so members that were planning on coming to their club for dinner. One such member was planning to celebrate their anniversary. We knew this member would not be satisfied with a buffet on this most special of occasions.

"So, one of our team members—our Concierge, placed a call to inform him of the situation. Needless-to-say, the news was not met with a happy response. Although our team member had anticipated the potential for such a response, it still was disappointing to the Concierge who had the foresight to recognize the need and make the call.

"Our Sommelier saw that his team member was upset and he suggested she go a step further. Together they planned the recovery. She made reservations for the member's special occasion at a beautiful restaurant downtown. She called to inform him of the newly laid plans and when he realized the effort she had expended to help him, he was emotionally touched. He was apologetic about being upset and explained how special the night was to be.

"Shortly after the call was made the wonderful power returned. We were able to fulfill the evening and not offer the buffet at all. All of our members were very happy. Our anniversary couple was so pleased they even wrote a formal letter of thanks to me which I passed on to the team. I love that our two team members found a way to embrace their empowerment—take action and save the relationship."

When an individual unwraps his or her gift of empowerment and takes action to keep the organization *balanced*—she leaves tracks. The tracks are going the same direction as the rest of the pack—toward success, but they are individual tracks. In the instance above, she made her contribution—and she knows it! She added to the success of the whole. And for that moment in time....she leads. Therefore she is a leader. And no title was presented.

How do we instill in a culture the *Find a Way* mindset?

→ Empower individuals to think and act.
→ Define a playing field so they know their boundaries and feel safe inside of them.
→ Transparently share the real goal of retention of relationships so each knows where to aim.
→ Reward and celebrate when the goal is achieved. Share the success.

Then creativity and a tenacious quest to overcome and emerge victorious will drive the individual.

He was *just* a player—a High School Junior. He pushed himself hard in the weight room. His personal goal was to squat 600 pounds. He was on track to achieve his goal. Each day he would complete his reps and then return to the circuit to help encourage the others to do the same. It didn't matter if the coach was present or not—on his watch there was no slacking on reps...not cutting back on weights. He knew he was just a player and so did everyone else. But somehow when the 6'2" 240-pound lineman said to keep pushing and finish strong they did.

The next year he was named Captain.

His tracks led to a title.

Did the Captain have influence because he was the Captain? Or did the being *just a player* have influence and become the logical choice for Captain?

Leaders leave tracks and those tracks lead to a positive place of change. Those tracks turn into legacy.

🐾 🐾 🐾

A few years ago, I was preparing a speech for the *National Association of REALTORS* in Washington, D.C. It was entitled *Lessons of Leadership from the Dirt Road*. I interviewed respected leaders throughout America. The common denominator among each of these leaders was their starts happened along America's dirt roads. They had humble beginnings....Patricia Diaz Dennis from *SBC Communications*, Len Dawson from the *Kansas City Chiefs*, Dr. James Neff from the *University of Nebraska Medical Center Orthopedic Oncology*, Ted Miller from *Dolly Parton Productions*, Marsha Johnson Evans from the United States Navy and Girl Scouts of America, and many more. I asked each interviewee one question: "What did you learn about leadership growing up along America's dirt roads that you have never walked away from in your professional life?"

One great interview was with the now deceased Millard Fuller—founder of *Habitat for Humanity*. When I asked him the question, he paused, taking time to think. Then he smiled. It was a warm reflective smile. His sweet, low, slightly Southern voice spoke,

> "Well, I could never run away. Growing up along a dirt road meant my momma could always find me. All she had to do was look for my footprints. I guess I have always worried about what my footprints say about me as a leader...where I have been and where I am going. Leaders leave footprints."

Leaders leave tracks.
Great leaders encourage others to leave tracks as well.

APPLICATION

1. Look at the gaps in behaviors. Identify areas where you wish you had more ownership of decisions and actions. Discover if all players understand the playing field. Are there empowering boundaries? Do they know decisions they can and cannot make? If not—create a well-defined playing field and communicate it.

    a. Reflect to see if you are making all the decisions and taking action. Maybe your behavior is stifling the actions of others. Remember, you cannot play the game on the field. Let go and let the players play.

2. Encourage each member of the organization to establish individual, personally motivating goals—but connect those goals back to mission and team success. Explain how the individual goals can only be achieved by helping the whole be successful.

3. Celebrate and internally market leaders who leave positive tracks, whether that leader owns the title or not. The behaviors to which you give a stage will be the most duplicated behaviors.

4. Purposefully celebrate individual actions that mastered obstacles and helped all stakeholders be successful. Establish a *Find a Way* mindset where overcoming obstacles and rising to the occasion is expected, celebrated, and honored.

5. Engage in one-on-one conversations about learning and how to improve empowered decision making that continues to balance the success of key stakeholders.

LESSON FOUR

Learn

Wolf Trait

Wolves have a very detailed education process. The breeders teach their young. Those young stay with the pack for two to three years to help their parents teach their siblings. The yearlings learn how to hunt and behave from their parents. A benefit of being in the pack is being the recipient of passed down learning…not having to learn everything 'the hard way'. For instance, some packs know how to hunt deer better—some hunt elk or buffalo. Some packs swim well, crossing a mile-wide river every day to hunt. A pack with a highway in their territory will teach pups how to read traffic and avoid people. The learning lives on and is passed from pack to pack as offspring venture out into their own worlds. No one starts from scratch.

Wolves are seekers and learners. Curiosity is their spark, often traveling several miles just to locate the source of a sound or a smell. Each day is centered on learning and application so they make life better. They have a yearning for learning.

It was the conference championship game. For 12 years the opponent had won the title. It was a quest...a true yearning deep inside each individual player—not just to bring home the conference title but to beat the opponent. The rivalry was intense. The coach prepared for the game just like any other.

He told a story of Tiny Focus.

Now this next point can be somewhat contradictory to what I have shared so far. We have talked about compelling visions and guiding missions; big pictures with 35,000-foot views. Now we talk about a process known as Tiny Focus.

> "If you worry about whether or not we are going to win this game," Coach Gosch began. "I know we will lose. But if you worry about the play at the moment and being committed to each play—one at a time, we stand a huge chance. Be your very best each and every play. If you do...either outcome—we walk off this field victorious."

That is Tiny Focus.

- → Understanding the intricacies of doing things right in the moment.
- → Being able to identify what is involved in the correct way and what is involved in the incorrect way.
- → Knowing what it takes to get it right over and over again consistently.

Coach Gosch explains Tiny Focus.

> "Don't get lost in the big picture. Focus on a tiny part of it and don't get distracted by the other stuff. When we cover a receiver, we tell them to focus on the inside hip only, not the whole man. Keep track of that inside hip. It is about limiting distractions."

There is a frequent saying among the Wolves defense coaches:

Our feet replace their feet.

Each Defensive End is taught to keep his hands on that Offensive Tackle and squeeze him down—drop the outside shoulder—work back up underneath that block and get downfield. Don't just rise head up and run downfield. Don't look at the goal line. Examine the components to success because details matter.

The Defensive End and his coaches may have four video clips where the actions of the player were wrong. Then, in the fifth clip, something magical happens. The player does it right! They don't study the four times. They study the *one* time. Each element of that right time is broken down. They look at feet and hands. Each component of *the right way* is viewed as if it was a cell under a microscope.

WHY?

Because being great isn't luck. It is purposeful and intentional. It is a series of right things connected together consistently to produce expected results of greatness.

Each player on the Wolves team has access to game film through the use of the service Hudl. Coaches spend the weekend reviewing film and making notes about each step of the performance. Players link to the video, review the notes, and prepare to discuss the learning each Monday after school. Each player is expected to review Hudl film at least 10 minutes each day. The review is first and then the coaches begin to share how to apply the reviewed learning for the next game. Every player gets a copy of the scouting report for the upcoming game. They see what the coaches see. They learn.

When understanding the difference between the right way and the wrong way is achieved, the coach's job becomes much easier. Each step is memorized. The player knows when he does it right and when he does it wrong. And one sentence yelled from the sidelines is all he needs to hear to get back into consistent process.

TINY FOCUS!

Each player is very aware that he is responsible for his own spot on the field and his ability to focus on that task at hand.

The Cornerback runs down the field in hot pursuit of the Wide Receiver. Everyone knows the Quarterback is throwing the ball to this specific receiver. He can feel it. He knows *his guy* is the target. So many thoughts…no interference, don't let him catch it, get there first, don't let him beat you deep, intercept…

There is just too much. It can be overwhelming. But in his head are two words, *Tiny Focus,* and he knows what he must do. Put a tiny, intense focus on his inside hip—his core…that way he knows which way the Receiver is turning and what he is planning on doing. He can fake out with his head, his eyes, his arms, his legs…but the belly—the core cannot fake out. Wherever the core is going is where the Receiver is going.

With that Tiny Focus, he never loses him. He stays tight and on task.

The front desk agent at a hotel is no different than that Defensive End or that Cornerback. He or she has a set of steps that must be done the right way to achieve the goal of a happy guest ready to embrace the journey to discover the room and engage in the hotel experience. Each must:

- → Prepare the work station to accept the guest.
- → Make eye contact with the guest prior to the approach.
- → Offer a genuine smile and appropriate tone of voice with the greeting.
- → Choose correct wording with the greeting.
- → Show mastery of the technology.
- → Deploy graceful speed of service.
- → Invite the guest to enjoy the experience.
- → Display sincere gratitude.

He or she must also stay in the moment and remain engaged with each guest.

Any one of those components breaks down and the guest satisfaction begins to decline.

TINY FOCUS!

In the movie *The Patriot* with Mel Gibson, there is a line "Aim small, miss small." I wondered what that line meant. It was an intriguing point in the script. I spoke with a marksman who trains police officers, utilizing firing ranges. He explained that if an officer is shooting to hit a whole man and misses the target, he or she will miss the whole man. But if he aims to hit something very small like the zipper on a jacket and misses—he is still effective in the quest.

TINY FOCUS!

On the playing field of customer service and guest experience creation. I often refer to this as *Moments Matter* or *One Moment at a Time*. Customer experiences are created in moments, not in whole days or whole events. In order to create memories or repeatable experiences, each service provider must master the moments.

What does this have to do with learning? Great leaders don't examine and critique whole days. They look within the moments that made up the day and pull up great moments of customer engagement. Leaders study moments and apply the learning into the next moment instead of making sweeping comments and commands about days or periods. Customer service providers can master moments. The customer only gives us moments of opportunity—not days.

Examine the pieces of the engagement, whether they be in the workplace or on the football field and find out the key steps that must happen so the experience will be successful for all involved.

Early on in my career with *Herschend Family Entertainment*, I learned that the friendliness of the Parking Lot Attendant directly influenced the ticket price. If the Parking Lot Attendant was welcoming, smiling, and helpful…the ticket price wasn't as bad. But if the Parking Lot Attendant made entrance and parking a real hassle, and the Tram Driver barked orders…the ticket price was often too high and not worth it. This unofficial research was collected through serving as Park Host over and over again—being called whenever there was a negative guest situation. Likewise, if the Ticket Agent at the front gate was crabby, the first Greeter at the entrance to the park had a tougher job. And if the Greeter was not on her game, the first troupe of Entertainers had a higher hill to climb to get guests to relax and have fun. Each position carried the guest from one experience to the next…handing off, just like passing a football with care. It takes a team.

When I started my own business, I was introduced to a master at the art of creating memorable guest experiences, Mr. Ted Miller. To say that Ted understood what it took to engage with people is an understatement. He is the Business Manager and Partner of *Dolly Parton Productions*. He co-founded *The Dollywood Foundation* and serves as Vice Chair. He also helped launch Dolly's literacy initiative, *The Imagination Library*, a book gifting program that distributes one book a month to children from birth to 5 years old. Imagination Library gifts over 10,000,000 books annually.

Ted serves on governmental and tourism boards, and lodging associations. Most recently he helped conceive and build *SmartBank* in Florida and Eastern Tennessee. *SmartBank* was born in January of 2006 with the compelling vision of becoming a bank with the image, values, and service levels incomparable to any other bank in its competitive set. In January of 2007, it opened in Pigeon Forge, Tennessee. Today, *SmartBank* has 12 branches in East Tennessee and the Florida Panhandle. A visit to *SmartBank* feels more like a visit to a friend's house with an invitation to stay for a bit and hang out in the living room.

I first started working with Ted when *Dolly Parton's Stampede* came to Branson, Missouri, in 1995. *Dolly Parton's Stampede* is an indoor themed dinner attraction featuring magnificent horses, talented riders, amazing singing and dancing, and a delicious four-course meal. They have locations in Pigeon Forge, Tennessee; Branson, Missouri; and a *Pirate's Voyage Adventure* in Myrtle Beach, South Carolina; and Pigeon Forge, as well as many other entertainment venues.

Like any skilled producer, Ted knew that a great show had cue points, staging, scripting. So, it was logical to him that the non-show elements of the *Stampede* had to execute at perfection, just as well as the actual show. A performer hits a mark on cue. So, too, a Greeter hits a cue when a guest approaches the entrance. A Horse Walk Attendee hits a cue when a guest asks a question about the story of a specific horse. The Retail Team knows their blocking and the Carriage Room Team understands what touchpoints they must hit to make the show inside of the arena more successful. Ted asked me to hone and personalize the wording for Branson's *Stampede* on a document known as *The 50 Steps of Absolute Customer Satisfaction*. Each touchpoint of the guest experience was described in its utopian state. We then were able to see the picture of the true desired outcome for each job. Leaders could coach to the specific touchpoint to ensure *Absolute Customer Satisfaction*

(ACS). Everyone knew their role in the show every step of the way. Each team member works daily to achieve a perfect ACS score. Tiny Focus.

Next, we took those 50 Steps and designed a training curriculum that is still deployed today.

More than once I have seen the leadership team of *Dolly Parton's Stampede* look at a guest comment that may be recommending improvement and go back to the 50 Steps to find where something broke down in the process.

It is much easier to manage moments than whole experiences. The tool of the 50 Steps is never about the tool as a document. It has always been and will always be about the guest experience. It is a way to give Tiny Focus to the massiveness of a 2+ hour experience.

I am forever grateful for my dear friend, Ted Miller, for teaching me that incredible lesson of intricate steps.

With that learning deeply embedded in my brain, I later created a process known as *The Seven Stages of a Guest Experience*© where we give *Tiny Focus* to each step along the way of any customer experience, whether the customer is engaging in a theme park, theatre, restaurant, bank, hotel, hospital, doctor's office, retail store. This universal template is a starting point for organizations wanting to instill the Tiny Focus concept into their operations.

When we dissect the experience into stages, we can then focus on each step and allow individual or team *ownership*. We can examine where we are strong and where we need work.

It is like a recipe to a perfect chocolate cake. We must have flour, sugar, chocolate, and eggs—and if one is left out or not measured correctly, the cake isn't right. Also, if the quality of the ingredients is not good—the cake doesn't come out perfect. So—if the baker puts in bland, white, stale flour the taster simply says, "That is awful cake!" He doesn't say, "The rest of the cake's ingredients were wonderful, but the flour just wasn't right."

Every little thing adds up to create one summation of a brand. And that summation turns into social media posts, repeats, recommendations, or bad reviews.

Tiny focus also leads to seamless execution and a holistically amazing product.

TINY FOCUS IN THE MOMENTS LEADS TO VICTORIES.

The spa at *La Posada de Santa Fe* is known as *Spa Sage*. It is an amazing escape into a world of relaxation and southwest elegance. White sage burns away stress and negativity. It is an immersive experience. During a consulting trip with the resort, I found time to explore *Spa Sage*. I discovered another learning point that supports the concept of being awake in the moments and mindful of the Tiny Focus.

There is a concept I refer to as *never take your hand off the guest*. It works so well in the world of guest service. I was the recipient of such style of service at the *Spa Sage*. Upon check-in, a receptionist welcomes and escorts the guest to the dressing area and then on to the Relaxation Room where the therapist picks up the guest and escorts him or her to the procedure room. Once on the table for the treatment, the Massage Therapist engages in the concept of *never take your hand off the guest*.

As a Therapist is massaging a client, the client begins to trust and relax. During the process, the therapist is using massage oils warmed by the hands. There is constant contact between the therapist's hands and the client's skin. When the massage oil is void, the therapist must get more oil. In most spas, the therapist leaves the client and takes her hands to the oil bottle, squirts the oil into her hands, rubbing them together and then comes back to the skin of the client.

When that happens, the client jumps ever so slightly because it is impossible for the therapist to return to the client and touch at exactly the same location on the body that she left. My therapist was different. She kept one hand on my skin at all times and brought the bottle to the touching hand, squirted the oil into the cupped hand on my back and returned the bottle to the side table without ever taking one hand off of me. I felt that ever present touch and security. Little tactic. Huge differentiation. Tiny Focus!

> Learning is far more valuable in a culture than knowledge.

Knowledge is given, but the process of learning is individualized and internalized. Organizations cannot learn. Organizations can have knowledge in the form of manuals and systems and processes. Individuals learn. Great teams are not great because their coaches have a lot of knowledge. Great teams are made up of learning individuals and knowledgeable coaches who put learning players in positions to try…and often fail and then try again and succeed. Great coaches in sports teams, as well as in business, put people in positions to learn and apply what they learn…again and again.

> Learning is doing…studying…applying…
> doing it again…studying…

My coach and mentor, Dr. James Belasco, wrote in his book *Flight of the Buffalo* about a leadership practice known as *FCLP: Focus Conversations on Learning and Performance*. More than once I sat in a room hearing him inquire—

> "What did you do?"

> "What did you learn?"

> "Now…how will you behave differently or the same because of what you learned?"

Look at the results…not activity. Examine what it took to achieve those results…good or bad. Have conversations about those results, the actions that got there and the learning. Then capture that learning in the form of examining individual actions. By doing these things, we will know how to apply it to get either the same results or better results. It removes the *cross your fingers and hope it happens* style of operation.

Dr. Belasco writes in *The Ten Commandments of Success*:

> "The future belongs to those who learn. I'm a learner first, second and third. The universe is my classroom, and you who share the road with me are my teachers. May I always have the humility to say, 'I don't know.' The commitment to say, 'I'll find out,' and the friends and supporters to say, 'I'll help you do it.'"

> Learners are seekers.

We learn from doing but we also learn by asking others to advise us. Football Coach, Ross Griffith, from West Valley High School in California shared a perfect example of this desire to get better and better.

> "I remember being a player for Coach Lance Gosch at West Valley. The defense would work hard all through practice and then you would hear Coach Gosch go up to Coach Grandell, the head coach, and ask, 'Hey did we look okay today?' And he would dig a little deeper, 'Are you sure? Am I looking at everything?' I always thought that was weird that he would ask for criticism. As a high school kid—I couldn't imagine wanting to be coached more than I already was."

Then Coach Griffith smiled as he reflected on his own current style as a coach.

> "It wasn't too long after I had been appointed Defensive Coordinator for West Valley when I did the exact same thing. I was totally into this practice. It was the last one before our big game. I had been deep into the details of the practice. When we were done, I walked right up to Coach Grandell and asked, 'Did we look okay today?' He just smiled and said, 'Your defense looked great today. Everything is going to be okay.' And then, I will never forget, he just smiled at me and called me 'Lance.' It was a great compliment."

It is not only the player or entry level employee that learns. The leader learns as well, and by demonstrating that passion for lifelong learning, we create a culture of learning and a team of learners.

> Ask for input. Value it. Apply it. Be thankful for it.

Sometimes we don't ask for input or learning, but it still hits us up the side of the head and screams, "Wake Up!"

During my reign in Marketing for the *Silver Dollar City Theme Park* in Branson, Missouri, I was asked to champion a task force to design the key appeals of the first children's festival. I was young. I didn't have any children. I didn't hang out with people who had children. I wasn't related to any young children. So, my colleague, Charlotte Davidson, and I *rented* a bunch of children.

Our target age range was 5 to 11 years. We turned to daycares, preschools, church groups, and individuals, and acquired access to about 60 children. Over the course of several weeks we would gather them and tell their parents,

> "We are going to pair your child up with another child and a chaperone. We are going to let them 'do' the park the way they want to do it…go where they want to go and see what they want to see. We are going to let them eat what they want, so we warn you…we will sugar them up and give them back to you. We are giving them each $20 to buy something they want as a gift. We are also going to give them a disposable camera. We want them to take pictures of what they see."

It was a grand adventure. One little boy, however, taught me a lesson I will never forget. It has guided my entire mindset about customer experience creation, and service ever since.

Board presentation day arrived. I had my storyboards and concepts ready to go. I was presenting our final recommendations for the festival. There was one last roll of film (yes—film was cased in rolls in those days) still waiting for me to pick up at Wal-Mart. (yes—we had to develop film and get real pictures.) I stopped by the store on my way to the meeting. In the parking lot, I opened the envelope of pictures and discovered 36 exposures of rear ends! I couldn't believe it. Every picture in this boy's camera was spent capturing people's backsides.

I had to call his mother. *What in the world was wrong with this kid?*

When I told his mom about the pictures she called him to the phone.

I began, "Honey…I am so curious. I asked you to take pictures of whatever you wanted to…and you took pictures of people's bottoms. Can you tell me why?"

His answer was abrupt and without compromise. "Lady! That is not what you said. You told me to take pictures of what I see. I am six years old. I am short. It was crowded. I SEE BUTTS!"

My paradigm didn't shift in that moment…it catapulted to a new dimension. All the activities we were proposing were street level…clowns, parades, face painters, chalk artists, balloon artists, street performers. Nothing we were layering on for the festival was going to hit the target audience. They were not going to be able to see it. Dad was going to have to pick up his kid and put him on his shoulders just so the child could see what was intended for him all along.

And it took a very smart little six-year-old to teach us that…

KIDS SEE BUTTS!

That year we spent more time designing risers with signs that read, YOU HAVE TO BE UNDER THIS TALL TO CLIMB UP HERE. And it featured a ruler measuring height.

We also put themed, brightly clothed characters on stilts and elevated performers. We hung beautiful decorations from trees and put various décor elements on all levels. All thanks to our young teacher.

I stood as Facilitator for a *Big Cedar Lodge* Executive Leadership meeting. The team was identifying their core values and pillars to success. For two hours, we discussed the importance of *learning* as a cultural foundational pillar. The word knowledge had made it onto the table. But it didn't capture the true behavior. *Learning* is far more important for a leader to inculcate. Knowledge is static.

Learning…applying…learning again.

It is how any pack survives and embraces change.

APPLICATION

1. ENGAGE non-operational partners to help you see the experience of doing business with you. What steps do they take? Be a student of the process and identify the main steps that must happen to achieve a successful execution of your operation. Break those steps down into *key ingredients* (steps).

2. TEACH—walk all those who touch those steps through the *perfect execution* of each step so everyone can see how the elements come together to create success.

3. EMPOWER—let those closest to the doing *own* the steps.

4. INSPECT—EXPECT—REFLECT. Keep looking at those steps—don't run off and focus on something else. Stay true to the plan. Expect excellence every time. Reflect on the process when it works and when it doesn't. Apply the learning.

5. FCLP—Focus Conversations on Learning and Performance. Ensure you take time to have conversations about results, learning, and application of learning after each major finish line. Focus on the application of learning to improve results. Let the doers engage in their own learning…don't just pass on knowledge—let them learn.

6. INCENTIVIZE a kid to tell you what your world really looks like! Or…ask a customer who has a pure heart and nothing to gain. Honesty will flow.

LESSON FIVE

Communicate

Wolf Trait

For wolves, the key to social interactions and success is good communication. They are holistic communicators, using much more than just their voice to be heard. To be more assertive, they make themselves appear larger…standing erect, ears and tail tall, eyes forward.

Howling back and forth is done inside the pack. It is executed to show support. It also is used to signal time for rendezvous. Wolves howl to locate one another. A distinctive howl is the one that warns, "Stay away—this is my territory."

When a pack has been sleeping, the Alpha Male and Female rally the pack, assemble them, and start the daily howl. Each must join in or be nudged by the Alpha. Through howling the whole is formed and engagement is in check. Heads raise, tails wag, the mission lives.

I stand before audience after audience…health care, entertainment, education, retail, banking, hospitality, real estate, manufacturing, government…asking one question, "What do we need to get better at around here?"

The answer is always "COMMUNICATION!"

We love to know. We cannot get enough!

But why is having enough communication in an organization such a mountain to climb? I believe it is because most people think communication is about *telling*. But really…

Communication is about *sharing*!

If Effective Communication had a synonym it would be Shared Understanding.

When shared understanding is achieved, respect grows. When respect grows, results improve. When results improve, opportunities increase. And the world changes for the better.

Communicating with the heart to serve and empower is respectful.

> The true goal of the leader's communication is to have information received and understood in the manner it was intended.

When this happens, the communicator learns more along the process, applies that learning, and continues the dialogue. Communicating is not a task on a to do list. It is not about sending the email or typing the text, placing the call or writing the memo. It is about ensuring all those involved in a situation have the information they need to deliver great performance. And that is not a one-way street. The *read receipt* option on email should be destroyed unless it is to cover thy rear end for a legal reason. Just because someone got it doesn't mean he read it or even began to understand its true meaning.

Communicating isn't a task any more than kissing is a daily exercise requirement for the lips. We don't communicate just to have something to do. We communicate to be effective, to raise awareness, cause passionate action, incite movements…

I had the privilege of coaching two leadership team members as well as the owner of *Porterfield and Company* from Harrison, Arkansas. This organization is a CPA firm providing accounting, auditing, and advising services. Tom and Susie Porterfield are the owners of this firm as well as the accounting service, BeanCounterFarm.com. I wanted to make mention of a behavior habitually brought to life each day within this firm. There is an overgrown white board in the center of the office. It contains a list of To Do items. It is a monster. Based on the ominous size of that board it could become an elephant in the room. Imagine coming into work every day and seeing a To Do list that will never go away. It can become oppressive.

But the leader *interprets* that board. Could the word *interpret* be a synonym to the word *communicate*?

The leader at *Porterfield & Company* consistently begins the daily stand-up (huddle) with an interpretive sentence. "Let's look at these tasks and identify how completing them is going to improve all of our lives."

And the white board becomes a series of stepping stones to a compelling vision! It is not a To Do list task master.

Coach Lance Gosch explains the Wolf Pack view on communication.

> "I think the quickest way to fail in communication with the team is to make it about you. I don't like to hear coaches talk about 'my offense' or 'my defense' to players. Bottom line is, it is not 'mine'. It is OUR team. We are going to get a lot more from our kids if they understand and believe it is their team and the success or failure of it rests in their actions and efforts. Communication is never one way."

At the beginning of each season, the Wolf Pack team of coaches select a leadership group comprised of 8 kids. Over the course of several weeks this team begins to discuss ideas, the Mission, and goals. The team collectively finalizes the summer workout calendar and the formal methods of communication are determined. Getting information out in front of everyone is key. More buy-in comes when others' time and schedules are honored.

> "We get the information into the hands of parents and players as early as possible to help with scheduling of players' work time and family vacation time in the summer."

Being informed about schedules that impact lives makes everyone feel a true part of the team and served versus being a victim to someone else's knee-jerk scheduling. A sense of belonging, responsibility, and empowerment surfaces.

After the ideas and goals have been culled, the leadership group presents them back to the whole team. The Leadership Team shares the Mission and explains to everyone why it is important and how each must bring it to life. This is especially critical to those entering the team for the first time. This *howling* sets peer-to-peer expectation early on.

A poster of the Mission and goals is produced and placed on a prominent wall in the locker room. Next to it hangs the summer calendar, so everyone knows the expectation of the schedule. In addition, all this information is posted on the team web page. The necessary steps and requirements to achieving *Iron Wolf* status are also shared.

Right after the regular school year ends and before the rush of summer begins the coaches call a parent meeting. This is viewed as an investment meeting. The more time and energy invested in this meeting the more returns in the form of buy-in and support are willingly given throughout the season. In the parent meeting the following is communicated:

- → Schedules
- → Expectations for attendance, behavior, attitude (from the players, parents, and coaches)
- → The coaching philosophy
- → Appropriate methods of communication throughout the season
- → Appropriate topics of conversation during those communications
- → The Iron Wolf Challenge requirements
- → Opportunities to get involved with Booster Club or Home Meals
- → Appreciation and praise for being a valuable part of the equation

Then question-and-answer time begins and two-way communication is encouraged and celebrated.

Before the first official practice, a team meeting is called. This is one of the most powerful meetings of the whole year. It is a clean slate meeting. The vision of the finish line is new and the line of site is clear. It is a *rally* feel where *anything is possible* hangs heavy in the air.

Each athlete stands, starting with the seniors. One by one they approach the Mission Statement/Goals poster designed by the leadership team and themselves. They sign it.

It is a powerful statement of buy-in. Each name stands visibly like the signature on a contract. It screams, "I WILL!"

As each signature is placed, high fives fly around the room. Hugs. Handshakes. A contract has just been made.

This contract stays up all season. And the leadership team often refers back to it. Huddles form around it. Seniors point to it when an underclassman loses his way. The words are alive because of communication.

The Keeter Center at College of the Ozarks in Point Lookout, Missouri, is one of the most unusual destinations in the world. The *College of the Ozarks* was founded in 1906. It charges its students no tuition. Each student works on a campus job to provide for his or her own tuition and expenses. It is a Christian, liberal arts college located on a 1,000-acre campus. Christian values, hard work, and financial responsibility form the foundational core of the *Hard Work U*-experience. One of the greatest recognitions for the college came in 2015 being named #1 Best Value College in the Midwest by *U.S. News & World Report*. They have repeatedly received this award.

The Keeter Center is a hospitality mecca at the entrance to *College of the Ozarks* housing the *Program of Hotel/Restaurant Management*. When guests stay at the hotel or have a meal in the dining room, students from this program are directly engaged in making the experience memorable and differentiating. It is a four-star lodge, restaurant, and conference facility.

The Keeter Center is world renowned for its *Community Convocation Series*. Many amazing leaders, such as Lady Margaret Thatcher, Secretary of

State Colin Powell, General Norman Schwarzkopf, President Gerald Ford, President George W. Bush, Tim Tebow, Senator Bob Dole, Senator Elizabeth Dole, and many others grace the stage at the Center's auditorium to deliver messages of guidance, hope, and leadership.

The Keeter Center's rustic design and beautiful furnishings stand as a jewel in the Ozark Mountain Country crown. The *Dobyn's Dining Room* prides itself in serving some of the finest dining the region under the direction of Chef Robert Strickland. Fifteen beautiful-decorated hotel suites provide an elegant escape unlike any other in the world.

And *The Keeter Center* is staffed by the students of *College of the Ozarks*. It is a living classroom in the disciplines of human engagement, hospitality, and leadership.

I have the privilege of working with Tom Healey, General Manager of *The Keeter Center and Guest Destinations*, and his team in the design and execution of a foundational concept known as GATE.

GATE is an acronym for Great Attributes To Embrace. We identified seven cultural pillars that are consistently critical to keeping the experience *at excellence* at *The Keeter Center*. When the team member deploys the behaviors associated with these seven attributes, the gate opens for all guests to engage in the amazing experience.

Tom Healey describes the significance of this program:

> "The G.A.T.E. program provides the cultural foundation for how we serve one another and our guests. By identifying the seven key attributes, it takes the abstract of work ethic and character traits and creates a dialog for staff engagement and personal development. The daily commitment to discuss a 'key' and the practical applications with the staff is what brings each attribute to life and creates an engaging environment with the staff and guests."

Each day, twice a day, at 9 a.m. and 4 p.m., the entire team at *The Keeter Center* engages in a GATE Meeting. This is a 10- to 15-minute stand-up meeting focused around one of the seven attributes. It is led by both leadership and select student employees.

The attribute is openly discussed and idyllic behaviors are showcased. The exchange creates awareness of the inner workings of the operation and allows staff members to understanding the purpose and overall objectives of each department. It is understood that everyone is working together for the same bigger goal of positive guest outcomes. During the meetings, positive guest feedback is celebrated, team member birthdays are honored and operational information is shared.

The GATE meetings are high energy, positive, passionately attended and culturally significant.

The GATE program is highly valued. Tom explains:

> "The GATE program was the fuel to take the operation from good to great, by setting the standard for how we provide service and develop our staff. Without the program, we would have a culture without a purpose…no roadmap to success. It is the most important thing we do each day."

Once, during an afternoon GATE meeting, a restaurant server shared about how she served a couple celebrating their anniversary. It wasn't until the conclusion of the dining experience the server discovered the couple was waiting to check-in and were celebrating their anniversary. The server invited them back for dinner and explained she would be happy to prepare a special celebration dessert for them. When she shared this story at the GATE meeting the whole team got behind her efforts and went to work making it a celebration to remember for the couple. Guest Services team created a special rose petal turndown service. The Culinary Team created special in-room amenities, and the Server wrote a handwritten note congratulating them and placed it with the amenity. All of this was to be in place when they returned to their room after the 7 p.m. dinner reservation. Unfortunately, the guests did not make the dinner reservation because they got delayed in traffic, but the staff proceeded with the in-room surprise. When the guest returned at 9 p.m., they went straight to the room to find a thoughtful note and special presentation. The guests became so overjoyed, they went to the restaurant to find the Server. She was working hard at her closing duties. The guests began to cry with joy because of the Server's actions from a simple conversation at lunch. Then, the wife hugged the Server and explained the emotion involved. She could never imagine a more thoughtful experience to celebrate their anniversary because her husband had cancer and might not live another year. Once this was explained the Server teared up and gave the wife a hug. Without hesitation, the Server asked permission to pray with the guests. The next day, this story was shared during another GATE meeting and everyone felt the joy of being a part of such a meaningful engagement.

Does this kind of focused and purposeful communication work? Well...only the nation thinks so! The online travelers' site, *TripAdvisor* ranked *The Keeter Center* No. 1 in *Top 25 Small Hotels in the U.S.* and No. 10 in *Top 25 Hotels for Service in the U.S. TripAdvisor* recognizes the world's best hotels with the *2016 Travelers' Choice* awards. Today, *TripAdvisor* still has *The Keeter Center* as the top *Traveler's Choice* and a *Top Small Hotel in the U.S.* And *Dobyn's Dining* carries a dominant *5-Star Rating*.

It really doesn't get any better than that.

If there is a daily huddle or stand-up like the GATE meetings at *The Keeter Center* or the Huddles in Hospitality, then team members begin to know that they will get the information they need at that set time and, if they have additional questions, that is the time to reach clarification. Weekly leadership meetings and posted minutes are always a tried and true way to stay on strategy and share results.

For the Wolf Pack at Reeds Spring High School, every Monday practice the scouting report for the week is distributed. Game film is watched. And each player is told everything the coaches know about the opponent and specifically the opponent that the individual Wolf will be playing against. Knowledge is power and the coaches spread the power to increase opportunity for success. Learning takes knowledge to the application stage. But it all begins with effective sharing of information...Communication.

Transparency is a needed cultural ingredient in today's world. Each must know how well we are doing on our journey to delivering great performance. So, weekly or monthly measured goals are shared. Budget numbers are transparent. Posted job openings, learning opportunities, customer comments, celebrations, monthly action plans... Information is like oxygen. We can't just get one hit of it a day and be okay—we need it throughout all the days' moments.

Formal communication needs to be others-centered and must include engagement. In all formal communication, we should see how this information is helping us successfully achieve our *Vision* while working congruently with our *Mission and Values*. In other words—*how* we communicate formally and *what* we communicate formally match the culture…not conflict with it. As an example, I once worked with an organization that talked a lot about core values and mission. The documents were posted everywhere throughout the buildings. Employees could quote them and were incentivized to memorize the words and spout them out on command.

Once a month the Executive Leadership Team would meet and review budgets and milestones within strategic initiatives. Never were those meeting minutes posted or shared. The monthly meeting took on a brand that included definers such as secrecy and negativity. Associates felt controlled by the conversations that were happening in those meetings but, in reality, no one knew what was actually happening behind those closed doors. So, the legend grew.

One day a memo was distributed right after the meeting. It was a short document with a *need-to-know-only* flair. It read, "Effective immediately, Joe Smith will no longer hold the position of Director of Operations. Executive Leadership Team will review the open position requirements and post additional information as it becomes available. All of us wish Joe the best of success in his new endeavor."

Now the reality behind this memo was that a wonderful guy, who I have named "Joe", had the opportunity to take a phenomenal job back in his and his wife's hometown. They were both ecstatic to be returning home and elated to be raising their three young children in their hometown. He had loved his job with our company and everyone was thrilled with his work. He was a true cultural fit. But this opportunity was just so amazing he had to take it. It was *immediate* because was he had given his resignation to the Executive Leadership Team and they were honestly happy for him. They knew he wanted to get started moving right away before the peak season of his new business was underway, so they waived his two-week notice and he agreed to help the transition virtually. The second in command in his department was very strong and could take the lead.

Even though everyone was saddened to see him leave our company, each knew it was the best thing for Joe and all were happy for him.

But when the brand of secrecy and controlling omnipotent power is associated with a formal standing meeting such as the Executive Leadership Team meeting and a *need-to-know* style of heartless communication is delivered—the story becomes something far away from reality.

The story in the break room mushroomed with words like, fired, no severance, walked out by Human Resources, his poor family, jerk Executive Leadership Team, I don't want to work for a place like this. *Poor Joe* dripped from everyone's lips. Anger and animosity over firing Joe became palpable. Even when the truth began to leak around because of one-to-one conversations with Joe or other Executive Leadership Team Members, few believed it.

With a little more *transparency*, that whole incident could have been prevented. We don't want to live in a need-to-know-only world. It is respectful and inclusive to share knowledge and pass on positive stories with flair. Jack and Jill went up the hill to fetch a pail of water. We know he fell down and broke his crown and Jill came right down after him. But wouldn't it have been nice to know that he was okay, and they went back up together to get the water and everyone had a nice cold glass of water with their meal?

Purposeful communication can be categorized into three circles…each one bigger than the next.

In the Executive Leadership Team example with Joe:

Must Know: Joe is leaving the company.

Should Know: He is resigning because he has accepted another position out of our community. Mark, the second in command in Operations, will be assuming the leadership role in the interim. We are happy for Joe and his family.

Nice to Know: He and his family are very happy. This job is in his hometown and the family is looking forward to returning home. He will be working with our company virtually to help with the transition as Mark is very capable to lead.

I believe it is the *Must Know* that keeps our doors open as businesses. It is the *Should Know* that helps us achieve our goals. It is the *Nice to Know* that emotionally links us and confirms that we are working for the right company performing meaningful work. It is the *Nice to Know* that makes us feel a part of something bigger than ourselves. *Nice to Know* is a strong retention tool.

Here is another example from my *Phoenix Home Care and Hospice* team that drives the point home and shows us how important it is to share knowledge.

The Intake Department accepted a new home health care client. The Scheduler needed to match a Registered Nurse with the client.

The Scheduler calls the RN. *Must Know* would sound something like this:

> "I have scheduled you with Mr. Jones. It is a Monday through Thursday assignment, 8 a.m. until 7p.m. He is a paraplegic and has a tracheotomy."

Should Know would sound something like this:

> "His first name is Bill. He likes to sleep late so he will not be awake when you arrive. Do not wake him for his meds until 10 a.m. and he will be much happier throughout the day. He has trouble with one of his pills. It is best to cut it in thirds and stay with him while he swallows each one. Use just water when administering. He chokes more on milk or acidic juice."

Nice to Know would be more like this:

> "Bill served in the military for 25 years. He fought in active combat in Korea. Some of his health issues are related to a war injury. He loves to watch John Wayne war movies on TV and he is honored when you ask him about his service."

When *Phoenix Home Care and Hospice* takes the time to share all three circles of information with their Caregiver, everyone is more successful on their journey to great performance. Bill is happy and tells his doctor that he is happy. Bill's family is happy and tells the neighbor to use *Phoenix Home Care and Hospice*. And they all live happily ever after.

In Kansas City, I was teaching a team of *Phoenix* leaders the three circles when a very bright young leader raised her hand and asked a very important question, "Which circle is most important?"

My quick answer was of course, "All three are important." Then I reserved the right to get smarter and thought about it again. "Each circle has a significant purpose. They are all important and they support one another—not as silos. But I truly believe Operations relies on the *Must Know* circle. Culture relies on the other two. *How* is in *Must Know*. I must know how to perform the tasks required. *Why* lives in the other two circles. *Purpose,* or *why,* is key to cultural success. The three circles work together to deliver operations at excellence and emotional buy-in to the results."

The grapevine lives in every organization and on every team. There are leaders who try to cut it off from its roots and destroy it. There are others that try to use it and manipulate it. And still there are others that freak out because of it and stand afraid of it. Then the tail wags the dog.

But there is a better way.

How do we not let the grapevine of gossip and misinformation thrive? Look at it as outside noise. We cannot control outside noise. We cannot control what the family members say, what the press says, what the chatter is around the watercooler. But we must acknowledge that people crave information and knowledge and, if they don't get it, they will search until they find some.

So, how do we effect *outside noise*? By creating a lot more *inside conversation*. Talk about it. Put topics on the table. Don't be afraid to talk openly and transparently.

One of the clients I coach asked me a question during our monthly coaching call. There had been a public blow up between two senior leaders in his organization. One whole wing of the office saw and heard the encounter. The two involved had made the argument public. But they had taken the resolution behind closed doors. He asked me if I thought he should talk about it to the group. My reply was "Why not? They are already talking about it. Why don't you just join them and get them back on track to their purpose and compelling vision?"

When we get afraid to talk about what is really happening, we create mountains and elephants in the room. Put it up for discussion and kill it! Conversation can be effective bullets to stopping negative chatter. And the dog is once again lead by his own head instead of his tail.

> Spontaneous and informal communication is vital to the achievement of vision.
> It is a critical element in the purposeful and intentional perpetuation of a culture.

I pulled up alongside the football stadium. I was a few minutes early to pick up my son. The team was practicing on the field. The stadium tunnels echoed the coach's words like the walls of a deep cave. "Wounded Eagle 22—Wounded Eagle 22…on two."

A moment passed. And then one simple word followed. "Again!"

Then…the head coach made a cultural command. "Nobody stands and watches! Wake-up! We need your help. Everyone gives all they have to give!

Wow—what a great way to say, "Get your head out of your ass!"

> "We need your help."

As human beings, we are wired to help one another. And what he said—he really meant. It takes each team member to be at our very best. No watchers. Because the Mission was inclusive. Because each is a part of the whole. Because the formal communication supports the culture and includes statements of unity and accountability, the informal moments on the practice field are accessories to the message…supporting it, enhancing it, defining it, and bringing it in home.

The Defensive Tackle presses his knuckles into the dirt. The whistle blows and the drill begins. The Tackle to his right doesn't see the trap.

"Again!" The Coach commands with frustration.

And the process begins again. The Tackle to his right doesn't recognize it.

"Again!" The Coach's tone now begins to sink with a tone of hopelessness.

The Defensive Tackle stops. His knuckles don't hit the ground this time. They make fists of frustration as he turns to his peer with determination and focused intent. "You know this! It's a trap. We have done this over and over again. Get it right."

And on the seventh try the Tackle does it perfectly. The Defensive Tackle smacks the back of his peer with an *attaboy*.

Informal communication.

Powerful.

Mission-driven.

Led, not by title, but by the one who needs to communicate and the one who needs to know.

Every day before practice the Wolf Pack meets to review either practice film or game film. Tiny Focus is discussed and examined. Focused Conversation on Learning and Performance (FCLP) occurs. Progress is celebrated and given a spotlight. Correcting measures are spelled out. The practice plan for the day is shared so that players go into practice knowing what to expect. That way there is less standing around and the drills run much more smoothly. Communication allows for the smooth-running effective practice.

Now in the heat of the game, situational communication among all the Coaches is critical. Coach to Coach Communication is the differentiating tip of the spear among competitive football teams. The Coaches must be able to talk to each other during a game and know that their voices are being heard. Each Coach is seeing something different. Their vantage point is different. Some are standing down on the field on the sideline. Others are up high above a press box. Another is in the press box. One might be overhead watching the view from a drone camera. Each must know that what they are seeing and what information they can provide is valued. Coach Gosch explains:

> "For this to happen all the coaches need to know their voices are going to be heard and valued. We want each other to talk. We need each other to talk. It is never about who came up with the idea. It is always about getting things fixed and getting it right. One person can't see it all. We need all eyes and all minds."

I want to take this football analogy into the boardroom.

> We should not allow title and power of position to determine authority among our Leadership Team.
> Line of sight to the customer and ability to lead in the situation should determine the value of the idea or input being delivered.

Now Leader to Associate communication has a very common denominator with Leader to Leader communication: Respect.

Coach Gosch also explains the important task of communicating coach to player.

> "There is not one way to communicate with kids. Each kid is different and each situation is different. We must adapt our style in order to get our point across and ensure understanding."

The stereotypical locker room halftime *butt chewing* works sometimes and in some situations…but not in all situations. In fact, sometimes that same style of chewing can have the exact opposite effect if the Coach reads his audience incorrectly or doesn't take the time to gain the players' points of view. For one player, a Coach may need to get face-to-face, nose-to-nose, and speak loudly to get a message across. And yet for another it may only require a head nod and a serious stare.

> Socialistic communication doesn't work
> when striving to achieve greatness.
> One-to-one matters.

One of my clients shared a personal story of her son and the effect socialized communication had on him in his High School. Her Junior son showed up every day to baseball practice. Never missed a moment. Volunteered at every opportunity. Groomed the field on work day. Helped his teammates. Accepted the challenges placed before him. Worked out on his own time. Hit the goals set for him. Practiced hard and intently. Listened. Respected. Behaved as a Team Player.

The coach stood before the team three weeks before tryouts and stated, *"If you want to know how I think you are doing, come see me. If you need to know what you must work on to get to play on my team, come see me. If you are serious about getting playtime and being a vital part of our team, come see me."*

Now, based on our previous chapters there was a whole lot wrong with those sentences…but this chapter is about effective communication so we will stick with the story to support that!

Her son was first in line when the practice ended. He wanted to know what the coach saw.

"Coach?" He said. "I want to play on your team. I want a spot on varsity. What do I need to do? What do I need to work on?"

The coach replied, "What are you doing up here? You know you are doing well. Get back to work."

Her son smiled. He knew he had it. The Coach had said so. Hadn't he?

The day came for the Varsity roster posting.

His name was not on the list.

There was no communication as to why. No opportunity to speak privately to discover what happened. Communication was just a list.

Her son spiraled into a mental quagmire. He never totally recovered. He lost his spark for the game. His Senior year he chose track and field after eight years of playing a game he loved.

So—how could that have been prevented?

One-on-one communication.

A Coach or Business Leader has every right to choose who is on his or her team. There were probably very sound reasons why that player was not on the Varsity roster. He could have had weaknesses that accounted for it. Maybe there was someone better on the roster. This is not a discussion about whether he had the talent to play. No one is *owed* a position. Each *earns* the spot. Talent and skill rank in the performance world a lot higher than dedication and heart do. Even if the coach's words disagree with that statement—more-often-than-not, behavior does agree with it. This example is not about performance. It is about communication.

> Everyone deserves communication—one-on-one, positive, honest, and enlightening communication that fosters growth and learning.

Closing the communication door and hiding behind a posted document is not effective communication.

Remember, *coach* is a verb, not a title…*leader*—the same.

A large Northeast organization I work with in the health care industry did a one-question survey of its associates holding various positions throughout the organization. The one question was, "What is communication? Define communication."

The consensus on the part of all Leadership was a definition that reflected:

> "Sharing of information."

The consensus among the Line Level Associates was:

> "A conversation."

There is the reason we often answer *communication* when asked, "What do we need to get better at around here?"

There is a definite gap when the Leader thinks his or her job is to *pass on information* and the Line Associate thinks we are supposed to have a *conversation* about it.

Leadership gets confused and frustrated thinking, "I told them what I knew!" And the Line Level Associate gets victimized by thinking, "No one asked my opinion!" *All fail.*

I had the opportunity to listen to a CEO of a home health agency—competitor to one of my clients—speak to his associates recently. This organization had been on a steady decline in market share for three years and could not seem to find the source of the bleeding. I found the source when I heard one specific sentence utter from the lips of the CEO: "I honor you by telling you what I expect from you. Do what I expect, and we will succeed."

Mmmmm? Source = CEO.

How is anyone supposed to be successful? No autonomy? He is the single gatekeeper of knowledge.

Sharing of knowledge is important.
Arming employees with information is a necessary action.
Transparency is a foundational principle,
not just a best practice.

But two-way conversation is a cultural pillar necessary for success!

A Quiet Football Practice Is Bad.
A Quiet Day At The Office Is Bad.
A Quiet Dinner Table Is Bad.

So…what is the secret to effective communication?

Shared Understanding!

Being able to say what you want to say from a place of enhanced vision and knowledge while at the same time listening (both to the words and the actions) and assessing if understanding and acceptance is being achieved.

To satisfy the need to have steps to success I am including what I believe needs to happen to achieve *Shared Understanding*—or *Effective Communication*.

> 1. A plan for formal, scheduled communication that people can count on. A true source of valuable information that is needed for success. Example—a daily stand up.

2. A team of exemplary individuals who passionately and accurately carry the messaging from the formal communication channels into the informal moments.

3. Two-way communication. A purposeful approach by the Leaders of seeking information as much or more than giving information.

4. Leadership using the common language of the culture in teachable moments…not just in the formal meetings.

5. Respect for each member of the team and what he or she has to say.

Much of my career has revolved around the discipline of marketing. I have always said that marketing is:

> "Everything we do to put our thoughts, products, ideas, and tasks in the hands of others and let them take ownership."

A sentence often heard in Marketing 101 is:

> "No one buys what you want to sell. He buys what he places value on—and how it will enhance his life."

Well…communication is no different. No one really cares about what we want to say. He cares about what he puts value on, determining how it will affect his life.

Communication is Marketing

Words matter. Choose them wisely—as if you were being paid to create the best tagline or billboard message. Every word counts when trying to achieve true understanding of your message.

I am the mother of a Lineman. What do football Linemen do? They create holes. I am proud of my son when he makes a hole for the Runner to squeeze through. But when I sit in the stands so far away and yell at the top of my lungs in front of hundreds of people, "NICE HOLE!" I am not choosing my words wisely because shared understanding is not happening and I am not marketing the fact that my son just did an amazing job. Maybe…"NICE BLOCK!" is a better, more marketable, choice!

How do I know?

When yelling "Nice Hole" the looks I get from all sorts of fans tell me the interpretation of my chosen words was not my original intent! *Nice* and *ass* sound pretty similar when shouted from the bleachers!

Market your words to achieve the desired behavior. Market your words to achieve ownership of outcomes. Market your words to achieve understanding in the way it was intended.

I walked down the hallway of the school on my way to a Foundation Board meeting. One student—a football player—was messing around in the hallway with another student. A Senior class football player walked by and I heard the sentence that proved a culture lives.

"Don't be stupid. What if Coach Gosch saw you?"

Coach = A good marketer.

APPLICATION

1. What behaviors do you want more of? Choose some great words to convey what you want. Market those words internally. Have conversations about them often. Find those behaviors being demonstrated and have conversations about that.

2. Ask at least two people on your team, "What do you think about _____?" once a week. Think about what they say and thank them for sharing their thoughts.

3. Look at the communication tactics in your organization. When are your formal meetings? How often? Are they well attended? Are people excited to come? Make sure these formal meetings are not *sit-and-get* meetings where you do all the talking. Build in conversation opportunities. Are those in attendance learning things that will help them be more successful and more engaged?

4. What type of informal communication tactics do you deploy? When do you sit in the break room? Do you listen more than you talk? How often do you have pop up stand-ups? Are they fun? Do others get a chance to talk? If you answered "no" to some of these questions, just walk around.

Listen. Comment on positive things. Share some information and ask some questions. The world will change.

5. Your words are your marketing messages. What are you marketing?

LESSON SIX

Serve Others

Wolf Trait

A true secret to a wolf pack's success is found in a fully immersed childhood. In comparison to other animal families, the wolf pups grow and stay with their pack for a long time. The culture of learning and accountability grows—but an even stronger message is present…it is your responsibility to help out—to serve.

The strong feed the weak. The healthy nurture the sick. Those at risk are rescued by members of their pack. The lost are found. The young are taught. The old are taken care of until they die.

The wolf is a symbol of all things wild in the world. Their very presence indicates an ecosystem in balance…an ecosystem being served.

The scrimmage started out feeling more like an organized practice but soon it became as intense as a game under the Friday night lights. Competitive juices were flowing. Each was trying his very best. The play called was a Halfback draw. The snap.

Quarterback falls back. The handoff. The Left Tackle and guard make a hole big enough to drive a truck through. The Halfback dances through the canyon without even a brush from his well-trapped opponent. A few short seconds later he dances the tale of the victory in the end zone.

And then the huddle...Coach brought them in. He grabbed the face mask of the dancing Halfback and said, "Tell your Tackle, your Guard, your Quarterback and your Center thank you. They made that touchdown."

The face of the Halfback expressed shock. After all, he was the one that took the handoff and ran with skill and speed to the end zone.

The Coach saw the angst. "You carried the ball. But your Linemen made the hole that made that possible for you. And your Quarterback executed a great handoff. And your Center performed a perfect snap. *When you dance, you dance for them all.* Never forget it."

The ballroom at *The Hilton* in Christiana, Delaware, was beautifully dressed. Every detail was spectacularly attended to. Everyone's attire was their very best. It was a warm, summer night so the brightly colored, flowing gowns added color to the night. Crystal blue tones, hydrangea centerpieces, mirrored décor and twinkle lights conveyed the theme of *Shining Moments*. This was the *Mirrors of MJ Awards Celebration* for *Meyer Jabara Hotels*. What is a Mirror?

The *MJ Mirror Award* is presented to individuals within the *Meyer Jabara Hotel Company* who personify the positive company culture. Mirrors *behave* their way into receiving this award. They cannot just think about the culture or say the pretty words...they live it and demonstrate their belief behaviorally. For instance, if a person believes in one of the *Foundational Principles* of the culture such as *Change is Good*, then this person doesn't go about the day complaining about changes in operations. A Mirror would embrace the opportunity to learn and apply learning and adapt. The culture dictates that leaders are teachers. A Mirror would be a teacher during the workday…pulling up people and sharing best practices and new techniques.

Mirrors of MJ are nominated by peers as well as leadership. Nomination stories highlighting the actual behaviors are written. A panel of representatives read the nominations and vote on the finalists. Only a 100% *yes* vote will grant a Mirror!

Once a year, those selected as *Mirrors of MJ* are honored at a truly remarkable gala. The company puts on the best of parties to celebrate these recipients and their guests. The two owners, Mr. Richard Jabara, and Mr. William Meyer are always present and engage in the issuing of the awards.

Mr. Richard Jabara, co-owner and CEO of *Meyer Jabara Hotels*, took the stage for his opening comments. After he discussed the honor of being a Mirror and shared a message of the power of culture, he began to share his heart.

> "You know…I am a father. There is a wonderful feeling that happens when your child gets an award. You're sitting in the school auditorium and his or her name is called out as having achieved something wonderful. Your first thought is, 'Really? Have you seen his room? Do you know what a slob he is?' Then, your shoulders go back and your chin rises. You don't say it aloud, but you think, 'Yeah Man! That's my kid!' Goosebumps rise and for a moment you float just a bit above the ground. There is nothing as wonderful as seeing that earned joy on the face of someone you care so much about.
>
> "Well—that is how I feel on this night. Whenever Bill (Meyer) or I get an award in the industry—even at the national level—it feels good and we certainly appreciate it. Some we have earned. Some were just participation trophies. But when one of our own gets an award, the joy that I feel is ten times that of when I am recognized personally. My shoulders broaden, my chin rises, and I say to myself, 'Yeah! That's one of ours!'
>
> "Tonight, that feeling flows like warm honey. As each of the eighteen climbs on this stage and receive the *Mirror Award*, I float just a little higher off the ground. I am proud of you all."

When all we do is work for ourselves and live in a record keeping world of *in order to*, we miss out on our full potential. We miss out on *team*. So many go through life with the mentality of *I do this action in order to get this for myself*.

> But it is only when we altruistically serve others that we find the intrinsic reward of joy. We must lose the *in order to* and truly serve.

Adam is a wonderful and unique member of The Wolf Pack. He is a sturdy 6'1" Senior Lineman. He has worn the Wolves jersey with pride for four years.

Adam was placed into foster care at three months of age, very malnourished, and labeled as *failure to thrive*. His foster parents soon became *Mom and Dad* and a loving family was born. Love is the appropriate word to describe the relationships surrounding Adam. He is considered developmentally delayed and carries the diagnosis of Pervasive Developmental Disorder. But the fellow Wolves do not see *autism* when they look at Adam. They see *brother*.

Adam embodies the heart and soul of the game. He does not play a lot on the field, but he is fully engaged in every single moment. On the sidelines, he pats backs, offers hands up, helps when help is needed. And he cheers with the passion and heart of a champion. When Special Teams moments arise, there he goes…running out on the field as much a part of the success equation as the Quarterback. And the stands chant, "Adam! Adam! Adam!"

It is often the case, when Adam enters the field, that a fellow teammate meets him mid-field and guides him to his position. I have seen players face him in the right direction, take his hand and run with him on kick-off or kick-off return. And I always see the high-fives and chest bumps when he does well. I have seen fights nearly break out when an opposing team member grunts a derogatory comment about Adam. Always—always—I see that Adam is a treasured member of The Pack.

One of my favorite moments was in the Conference Championship game. Reeds Spring was ranked 4th among schools of the same size. We were playing a powerhouse monster school ranked 10th in the nation among schools their size…which was one division higher on the food chain than ours. They had taken the Conference Championship 12 times. They were big and obnoxious and acted as though it was a big deal to conquer us. They enjoyed perpetually dominating the smaller conference. For some, winning matters more than growth. But with just five minutes left in the fourth quarter, our little heart-filled school was ahead by 7! It was a David and Goliath moment. Then it happened. Their Quarterback threw the ball to a Receiver and our guy wrapped him up at the same moment as the catch. The ref called *pass interference*. It was a terrible call. Now I know every parent in the world loves to blame the officials. But this was blatantly wrong. It turned the momentum. Everyone in the stands was breathless. It was a huge penalty.

In the still of the awe one voice could be heard. It was Adam's. His hands rose in the air in disbelief and he loudly uttered one simple question, "What the hell?"

He said what every single person in the stands felt. His authentic heart conveyed what everyone else wanted to say.

His unfiltered heart continued to guide. Next, he did something brilliant. He turned to the stands—raised those same arms again and yelled, *"Who's got my back?"*

And the crowd stood with passion and the support of the Pack.

"I've Got Your Back!"

The back-and-forth chant continued for several minutes.

The Wolves didn't win on the scoreboard that night. But they won in every other way possible. And better men left the field.

And at the end of the season the Reeds Spring School Foundation awarded Adam with the *Heart of the Wolf* award. I had the honor of presenting. And the presentation read:

> "We have one more special award to present this evening. This is a premiere recognition. Our Foundation Board has never done this before. We adopted the opportunity this year because of one very wonderful student. Tonight, we announce the creation of the *Heart of the Wolf Award*.

"There are students that excel at grades, awards, the arts, sports, etc. and all students combine to make up the culture of a school. There are different cliques and clubs and tables in the lunchroom. But once-in-a-while there is a student that drives the culture...fits in everywhere he goes and makes everyone better for having known him. This student works to help. Volunteers. Is always present.

"The wolf is a proud and strong animal—others-centered, protective and nurturing. But the wolf also loves to play, is friendly and sometimes curious. The wolf is always—always—about the pack.

"I just have one hint to share who our winner is…"Who's got my back?"

"This year—the Reeds Spring School Foundation would like to honor our first Heart of the Wolf Award to Adam Gasper!"

And every member of The Pack took to their feet in acknowledgement and found *true joy*.

The greatest leaders in the world understand that to be leaders they must serve others.

Three important leadership questions for the other's-centered leader:

> → "What is great performance for you?"
> → "How can I help you achieve that great performance?"
> → "How can I help you remove obstacles that stand in the way of your success?"

These three sentences are not just thrown away brown-nosing questions used to fill space. These are critical inquiries taught to me by my coach, Dr. James Belasco. In his book, *Flight of the Buffalo,* he explains:

> *Great coaches in business help people see beyond where they currently are. Having the vision of 'great performance' is appealing.*
>
> *Often people don't see the relationship between their current assignment and their definition of success. The coach identifies that critical linkage. 'What do I need to do now to get there in the future?'*

That sounds a lot like *Purpose*. If I know *why* I am doing this today and *where* it is taking me, I do the doing with much more passion and conviction…because I have purpose!

The purpose of life is not to work. The purpose of work is to build a life. And on the journey of building a life we build relationships.

> Everything is about relationships.

The Leader doesn't look at the team and ask, "What do I need from them so I can be successful?" He/she looks at each member of the team and asks, "What does he or she need from me so they can be successful?" When the team wins, the leader wins!

When the team member truly knows that the Leader cares and the Leader behaves accordingly…the team member will do whatever it takes to be successful.

But if the team member believes he is busting his butt and grinding through the day just to make the Leader successful and the Leader is not lifting him up along the way—the martyr culture grows and the Leader becomes The Man that we all hate. Oppression begins.

Why really, I mean *really*, do I support the Coach?

Because he *loves* my son. And I believe that with all my heart. He truly wants the best *for* and best *out of* my son. And that is exactly what I want too. Not for himself. Not for me. But for my son.

When we honestly believe our leaders want the best for us and love us—in the agape form of love—we will follow them anywhere and take a bullet for them.

Kelli Gosch, Lance's wife, shared with me one day, "I just don't get it sometimes. The boys truly love this husband of mine. And he yells at them and makes them run and pushes them like crazy. And everybody loves him!" Of course, she was grinning when she said it. She knew exactly why they love him. Because he loves them.

Growing up under the wing of Dr. B has made asking these questions standard protocol. With the clients we serve, we engage in a process of writing annual *Performance Agreements*. These are equivalent to annual goal grids or one-year plans. These documents all center around the question of great performance. They are intimately linked to the *Vision and Mission*. With these documents as guides we are challenged with important questions:

1. What is *Great Performance* for the people you serve?

2. What do we need to do to help them achieve *Great Performance*?

3. How will you know when you have been successful?

That is such higher-level thinking than:

1. How much better do we want to do as a company this year than we did last year?

2. What expenses do we need to cut to get there?

3. What new business will we target?

4. How do we split up the nut to crack among our salespeople and assign percentages of growth?

The first example is others-centered service leadership and the second is self-centered management.

As Chairman of *The Reeds Spring School Foundation*, it is my job to secure the guest speaker at our annual fundraiser, *Pack Night at Dolly Parton's Stampede*. Our *Foundation* exists to raise money for college scholarships, believing the only way to positively change the world is through education. We strive to help every child who dreams of college have a launching pad to that dream.

I found an opportunity to book a fabulous speaker for our annual fundraising night. Mr. David Baker was named *President of the Pro-Football Hall of Fame* in 2014. He came to *The Hall* with a wonderful background in leadership having served as the Mayor and Councilman of Irvine, California, and as the *Commissioner of Arena Football* where he established the first-ever Mission Statement and Fan Bill of Rights in sports. Prior to joining *The Hall*, he served as the Managing Partner for *Union Village*, the first integrated health village in the world serving 1,500 seniors and employing over 17,000 associates in Henderson, Nevada. He played professional basketball in Switzerland and worldwide with the *Christian Basketball League*.

At 6'9" and nearly 400 pounds, he has a different vantage point on vision than most. He dreams big, thinks big and is a catalyst for big. And this is where my story of David Baker begins.

He raised big dollars for our *Foundation*. His big heart fell in love with our coaches, our football mission and character program and my family. His wife, Colleen Baker, has the biggest heart I have ever known and she, too, came to our fundraiser and helped us generate big dollars in our silent auction. When they left, our world changed in a big way.

It was roughly eight months after their visit to Branson, Missouri, when the Baker family invited our family to visit *The Pro Football Hall of Fame* in Canton, Ohio. *The Hall*, under David's leadership, was going through an amazing transformation with the creation of *The Hall of Fame Village*…a Disneyesque immersion experience.

We headed North. The Bakers treated us as VIPs. Our boys were in heaven exploring every inch of *The Hall*. It was a grand experience.

That evening, The Bakers invited us out to dinner at a local sports bar. It was NFL Playoff time. Denver was facing Pittsburgh and a whole bunch of amazing people had gathered for the event, each carrying an impressive title associated with football leadership. During dinner, Mr. Baker looked at, my then 16-year-old son, Connor and asked a challenging question, "Hey Connor, are the Wolves going to be any good this year?"

Now my husband flashed me a quick look. A little fear hid in his eyes. Anytime an adult asks a teen a question anything is possible. You never know what to expect…maybe a grunt, a nod or as simple yes or no. But when Connor opened his mouth, it was as if Coach had stuck his hand in his back like a ventriloquist and was speaking every word. He began a soliloquy about the strengths and weaknesses of the team and how many Seniors were lost, what was coming up and where they were headed. My mouth had to be wide open.

Then Mr. Baker asked him one more question and the world changed forever. "What is your biggest obstacle?"

And in true 16-year-old fashion Connor replied, "We suck in the mud."

What????? Did he just say *suck* to the President of the *Pro Football Hall of Fame* in front of all these important people?

Yes!

And David Baker, father of two football players—one the starting left tackle for the Atlanta Falcons—replied, "Tell me about the mud."

And Connor did. "Well, you see, it rains a lot in the fall where we live. We have a terrible field. It gets so muddy we cannot practice on it. Then, when game time comes, we play on it and we aren't used to sliding all around. We lose the ball, lots of fumbles and falls. Our field sucks! We always go into Districts ranked high so we get home field advantage. We don't want it!"

David looked right across the table at me and said, "Mom—we don't have turf?"

I chuckled with reality explaining the high population of poverty in our district, highlighting that if a turf bond issue made it on the ballot we would be laughed out of our county!

The conversation of turf stopped there and we began to get engrossed in the game on the big screens.

One week later, after returning home, my phone rang.

The rest of the story has many details and a thousand phone calls. But the jest of the story is that David opened his heart and his circle of influence. He made a few phone calls to the company that was getting ready to place eleven turf fields at the new *Hall of Fame Village*. There was a one-year-old field lying on the ground at the *University of Cincinnati*. It was going to have to come up because they needed a new one with soccer field markings. The field was for sale. David Baker worked out a deal that made turf possible for the students of Reeds Spring Schools.

These conversations were in February. On May 1 of that year we walked onto a million-dollar professional grade turf football field with a bright red fighting wolf logo proudly placed in the heart of it.

And the world changed for The Wolf pack. The community stepped up and funded a new electronic scoreboard. The attendance grew. The gate revenue and concessions revenue grew. The Booster Club granted $6,000 to the Foundation for college scholarships. And today, the circle keeps on going.

David Baker, his wife Colleen, and the entire *Pro-Football Hall of Fame* have a passion for spreading the story of *building character* that rises from the game of football.

The mission statement of the *Pro Football Hall of Fame* in Canton, Ohio, is:

> "Honor the heroes of the game. Preserve its history. Promote its values & Celebrate Excellence Everywhere."

There is a place in the middle of the Midwest, in a little town called Reeds Spring, Missouri, where every single person knows the mission of *The Pro Football Hall of Fame*. Their mission has come to life. And *Excellence* is being celebrated on and off an absolutely beautiful field.

The Pack celebrates the player who serves the greater goal. Coach Gosch explains:

> "Gage had played Fullback for The Wolves for three years. He even started as a Sophomore most of the season when another player was injured. He did a very good job for the team. Going into his last year we wanted to change the type of player we had at Fullback. We wanted to get a little more quickness at the positions and not rely so much on size. So, we moved one of our Halfbacks to Fullback to get what we wanted at the position. It had nothing to do with Gage doing anything wrong, just a change we felt would make the position better for the entire Offense. Gage had played FB most of his Jr. High and High School career and, as a result, he had always worn the number 44 on his back. He was #44! It was a part of his brand.

> "Gage enjoyed playing FB and all the stuff that goes with it…carrying the ball, scoring touchdowns, hearing his name over the loudspeaker. We were getting ready to ask him to give all that up to play the Offensive Line—not because he was not good enough to play FB but because we think it will make us better as a team. To add salt to his potential wound he would no longer get to wear his beloved #44.

"We talked as a staff about the move. We knew it was the right move for the team but it would all hinge on how Gage took the news. How he responded. He could be resentful, turning the move into a controversy and disrupting the direction the team was headed. Or he could understand what we were trying to do and embrace the move and how it could help everyone around him.

"As we talked with Gage, he was a little shocked at first—I think more so about the jersey number than the position move. But after we talked and explained why we wanted to do it, he did not say another word. He took the move and ran with it. He never spoke about it again, never turned it into something that could have split the team. He just played the game. And he played it very well.

"Gage went on to start for us on the Defensive side of the ball. He *earned All-Conference First Team* and set the school record for tackles-for-loss in a season.

"Gage was the perfect example of putting one's own personal wants aside for the good of the whole. He was also a great example of receiving rewards when you give altruistically to the greater cause."

Serving Others Has Its Returns

We have learned that the privilege of wearing the beloved Iron Wolf on the side of the helmet requires the player to complete tasks that equate to points. We know that many of those points are performance and attendance based. But Coach Gosch and his staff have also built in the concept of *others-centered service*.

The Varsity football player is held accountable to serve others. He visits the elementary classrooms and talks about the power of character and strength. He serves at the neighborhood recycling center to lessen the impact of waste in our environment. He runs the chains at *Mighty Mite* football games. He visits *Mighty Mite* practices and assists with coaching. If there is a fundraiser, he is there. If there is a cause, the Wolves Football team has a presence. On Halloween night, the Varsity players build a haunted house and entertain Pre-K through sixth grade students at a *Trunk or Treat*. Last Halloween, over 2,000 trick-or-treaters were positively impacted by the Wolves.

It is not only about what's done on the field that matters.
It is about serving both on and off the field.

Serving is a concept that is preached from day one of summer weights. And it carries over onto the field. Each serves by doing their part for the good of the whole…playing for the name on the front of the jersey, as Gage personified…not for the number on the back.

ALIGNMENT—ASSIGNMENT

On any given day, the winds blowing across the Wolves field carry Coach Gosch's loudly spoken command, "Alignment—Assignment!"

"When we talk football, we stress just a few things and two of them happen before the ball is even snapped.

Alignment—Assignment and Get Your Butt To The Ball.

It does not matter how big and fast you are. If you can't get aligned in the correct spot and you don't know what you job is, you can't help the team.

On the flip side of that, if you are always aligned right and know your assignment, it will give you a chance to make a significant play even if you are not the better athlete. You will do the task at hand to serve the team.

We can scheme and draw things up but if, as a group, we can't get aligned and know our jobs, we won't have much success.

Then when the ball is snapped, it is just about the amount of effort made to get to the ball on defense. On offense, it is about getting your guy away from the ball and making a pocket or hole or path for the ball carrier."

If an Offensive Lineman makes a hole and the Quarterback chooses to leave the pocket and engage in the wrong assignment, the Quarterback gets sacked and some non-knowing parent in the stands yells angrily to the Lineman, "You've got to hold your block!"

On Friday nights, not getting aligned properly and not knowing your assignment will get *you* beat before anything else. It will get the *team* beat!

The bigger picture here is still *serving others*. Often there is no glory in Alignment—Assignment…especially if your assignment is to pull or get in the way or draw someone else away from the ball. The loudspeaker is screaming some player's name that is on the opposite side of the field as you. But doing your assignment accurately and to the best of your ability is for the good of the whole and the whole celebrates. If everyone played for their own personal glory—there would be no glory for anyone.

It was a cold October night in post-season District play. Our Wolves were fighting hard. Two teams matched up well. My son was Left Tackle. He had a strong player across from him and when he was supposed to block him, he did a good job containing. But there were many plays where the play called for him to pull…leaving the guy and carrying out his assignment on a secondary player. More than once that strong opponent broke through the play and sacked the Quarterback. "Alignment—Assignment" required my son to appear as though he was *missing* his block. But, on the contrary…he was doing his job. The Offensive Coach was calling the plays. He was aligning properly and following his assignment according to the play.

A father in the stands that played the game *back in the day*, when the role of the lineman was to *stand up and hit somebody in front of you* screamed my son's name and turned to the other ignorant father in the stands to profess his knowledge of why we were losing the game…blaming it all on my son.

The mother lion in me envisioned claws and blood! But I chose more wisely. I walked to his side in the stands. Sat down next to him and calmly addressed him saying, "Please don't yell my son's name when your knowledge is so limited."

Of course, there was a response.

It's not important.

Why is it not important? Because it is *never* about the people in the stands. It is *never* about the parents. It is *never* about the opinions of those that have not invested eight months of their lives to be able to play for eight or ten games. It is only and always about the sons.

We should trust and remember—they are following their Alignments-Assignments. We should follow ours…which is to align our goals with their goals, and then to complete our assignments of loving and supporting and encouraging. *Nothing else!*

We serve our sons. They do not serve our egos.

SERVE THE TEAM

If the Hostess in the restaurant is grouchy and sets the guests at a table, handing them off with distain, the Server fails right out of the starting blocks.

If the Teller at the bank cannot remember a customer's name and doesn't make an emotional connection during a deposit, the customer doesn't think about the Loan Officer when it's time for the new mortgage.

If the Stock person at the grocery store blocks the aisle and the customer cannot find the canned peaches, the price of bananas is too high.

If the Parking Lot Attendant is grouchy, it costs too much to get into the theme park.

If the Nurse is modeling Nurse Ratched from *One Flew Over the Cuckoo's Nest*, the Doctor isn't very skilled.

Everyone must align to the end goal and perform their specific assignment.

I stood against the wall of the grand ballroom at the *Marriott* in Stamford, Connecticut. My arms folded across my chest like a coat of armor. My bottom lip protruding just a bit mimicking a toddler who could not have the candy. I was pouting.

For fifteen years, I had been the Lead Coach on what the *Meyer Jabara Hotel Company* called *Executive Sessions*. Twice a year the entire leadership team, consisting of roughly 100 people, would gather for a three-day learning retreat. It was an awesome time, vibrant with engagement and applicable learning.

Each session followed the same template for organization. Richard Jabara, William Meyer, and Dr. Belasco would conduct a conference call with me and talk about what types of learning and topics of discussion they would like to infuse into the meeting. Then they would assign to me six up-and-coming leaders that would form the committee to lead the way.

The concept was that the Teachers always learn more than the students. These committee members would deeply dive headfirst into the learning and emerge true champions of the topics. This committee would research the topics, adapt them to be applicable at the hotel level and then serve as Trainers, Facilitators, and Coaches during the sessions and real leaders after the session. My job was to coach this committee. I conducted hours and hours of individual and team conference calls. I would push and push and guide and pray! Preparing for the Executive Sessions would often take two months of intense work. On the final day and in the final moments of each session, I was exhausted, yet proud.

Every single time—for fifteen years, on the last day, in the last moments…the committee would take the stage for the wrap up. They would thank their owners and Dr. B. They would applaud the staff of the hosting hotel. They would graciously acknowledge their teammates' contributions and provide a personal testimonial or two about their own learning journeys.

And then they would demonstratively thank me. Often the sentences were, "We couldn't have done it without her." "She was our true coach—our friend." "She helped us see the big picture and kept us focused on the goal." And, always, the praise came with gifts. Flowers. Jewelry. Candy. Plaques.

But on this final day of this Executive Session in Stamford, Connecticut, the committee took the stage. They thanked the owners and Dr. B. They applauded the hotel staff. They hugged each other. Two testimonials of personal growth were shared. And then the

Committee Chair thanked everyone for coming and concluded with, "Have safe travels home."

I was not thanked or acknowledged in any way.

Wallowing in a fit of feeling sorry for myself, I had retreated to the back wall and was mentally preparing my exit. Enter Dr. Belasco. Joining me on the wall he bumped his shoulder against mine and warmly stated, "Best job you have ever done, my friend."

I immediately thought he was giving me the pity compliment, knowing that the committee had forgotten to recognize my contributions. My reply was less than appreciative and dripping with sarcasm, "Oh yeah—sure!"

He didn't flinch. His eyes still focused forward on the mini celebrations in the center of the room. "Best job you have ever done."

I was still oblivious. I really wanted him to go away and leave me to my wallowing. But he didn't so I replied again, this time a little more grateful, "Thank you, Dr. B. I appreciate it."

This time he turned and looked at me, making sure I looked back. "You don't get it."

Obviously! I didn't get anything! No flowers, no candy…not even a thank you!

He said it again. "You don't get it at all. This truly was the best coaching you have ever done with this team."

So, I had to bite. "Why do you keep saying that?"

He replied, "Because they think they did it themselves."

Never have I ever felt a greater joy in leadership. It was the best acknowledgement of my career.

Serve Others

Help Them See Great Performance And A Way To Get There

Remove Obstacles For Them Along The Way

Let Them Get There

Coach is not a title. It is an act. It is a verb.

Coach is what great Leaders do. And great Coaches help us see what we cannot see for ourselves. They help us identify the purpose behind our actions and contributions. They help us see who we all inevitably serve. They show us that by serving others we are served; by helping others achieve their success, we achieve ours.

In the fairy tale story of *King Arthur and the Knights of the Round Table*, we learn that the Mission Statement of utopian Camelot was carved in the center of the Round Table. It read:

> "In Serving Each Other We Become Free."

But it takes a great Coach to help us see that.

Coach is a description of a Leader that is earned, not given.

WANTED OR NEEDED?

How do we know if we are successful servant leaders who are *others-centered*? I have my own personal method of measurement. It is found in the difference between being *needed* and *wanted*.

A boss can be really needed. We need that guy to make decisions, run block, gather resources, guide, and tell. And that boss might be very effective and hit the success metrics. But if the team members believe they did it themselves, and credit each other for their successes instead of the boss, the Leader truly served. When the Leader serves by casting a compelling vision, setting up the playing field, pulling up the desired behaviors, ensuring responsibility, removing obstacles…he or she is wanted at the table—not simply needed.

When we WANT our leaders, we willingly follow them with head and heart.

We *want* people in our lives that help us be successful and add to our lives emotionally. We *need* people that provide and fill our necessities in life.

Are you wanted or needed at the table?

APPLICATION

1. We know when someone honestly has our back or not. If you mean it, shout it with all your heart from the mountaintop.

2. Think about someone on your team. Spend a bit of time discovering what *Great Performance* is for that person. How does he or she define success? What does he or she dream about? What are his or her life goals? What does he or she want to learn? Then think about your circle of influence and try to figure *one* thing that you could do to serve his or her goals, without expecting anything in return. Do it. Then ask yourself, "What did I learn?" "How did I feel?" "What were the results of this altruistic service?"

3. Make a list of your *key stakeholders*. Who must you partner with in the next 12 months to achieve success for your organization? Lay down all your predetermined goals. Just look through their eyes. Ask them questions. Discover what *Great Performance* is for them. What can you do to help them be successful in their organizations? Make those actions part of your annual objectives. Merge their goals with your goals and see the pie get bigger.

4. Think about someone you truly *want* in your life…not just need. Ask yourself, "Why do I want them?"

LESSON SEVEN

Play

Wolf Trait

Wolves play a lot. Den sites reveal old chewed up highway cones, empty plastic bottles, old deer horns, etc. Play is a safe way to learn. Wolf pups jump, bite, and chase each other and learn how to fight over toys made of sticks and horns. Play is a way to grow closer together while learning. Play will also diffuse conflict and release tension.

Play also happens in the pack to build trust. An Alpha will play with the other strong males in the pack and rough house around together. Then, in the heat of the hunting battle, that social bond kicks in and they fight for each other's lives. Play is a low risk way to learn about the strengths and weaknesses of those on your team. Leaders and strength shine in times of play.

It was so hot. Early August. The temperature hovered around 98 degrees and it was still morning. Each player was dreading the conditioning drill. The entire Wolves coaching staff took to the field with stone faces of conviction. Every boy knew it was going to suck.

In each Coach's hand was a black gym bag. Players only imagined what could be within. Maybe exercise bands for stretching, weights to carry as they ran, drill ladders., anything was possible.

The Coaches placed the bags carefully on the ground. Coach Gosch uttered only one word, "FIRE!"

And with the passion and excitement of a mischievous child each Coach reached in his gym bag and loaded up with filled-to-the-max water balloons. War began and the players scrambled like mice. Giggles. Screams. Laughter. Fun.

It was play time!

Play is an important activity in nurturing the health of a team. And *play* is firmly planted on the *Responsibility List* of any great Leader. There are volumes of research papers that site *fun* as an important ingredient to reduce absenteeism, lower turnover, improve productivity, and increase revenue. But, more-often-than-not, the Leader looks at *fun* as a splurge and not an investment.

What does *fun* do?

- → Develops bonds—builds *brotherhood/sisterhood*
- → Breaks down walls or silos
- → Shakes up the status quo
- → Creates stories to tell which help define the culture
- → Draws attention to the team—making recruitment easier
- → Involves everyone
- → Wakes up different areas of the brain and sparks creativity and problem solving
- → Allows members to try new things—assesses strengths and weaknesses when the stakes are low
- → Blows off steam and reduces tension and stress
- → Creates memories

Our first High School football season was over. Best ever up to that point. The celebrations had happened and the awards were given. The Juniors were getting ready to step up and take the reign during winter weights. Some had moved on to basketball. Others were working out on the winter baseball program. But Coach Gosch and his staff were still working on Packing!

It was time to have a dodgeball tournament—the utopian definition of *fun* for high-energy, testosterone-laden young men. Teams formed. Many of the students thought the Senior football players just didn't want to participate. They had not signed up. Maybe they just had *short-timer syndrome* and just wanted out. The chatter turned to that conclusion.

But the day of the tournament arrived and so did the Seniors. The Seniors had formed their own team. Their grand entrance was unforgettable. One dressed as Thor from *The Avengers*. Another wore a *Gladiator*-style loin cloth and helmet. Each donned a cape or chest armor. One had full *WWE* garb with lace-up boots.

The house roared with applause and laughter. And, of course, the superheroes took the tournament and the coveted trophy. Months later, the stories still circulated. A tradition was born. And the Juniors that year planned for their grand entrance during their own swan song dodgeball tournament.

Fun Matters!

Each year The Wolves engage in pure fun activities that are purposeful and intentional. There is the *Impersonate the Coaches* party where the players get a chance to act out as their revered leaders. *The Flash Ball* game is played a few times each season where a football is thrown to a player and each player can only take three steps before throwing it again on the journey to the goal line. The Coaches even play along. And twice a year there are crazy competitive flag football games where the Coaches sit down and simply enjoy watching…with their mouths shut.

On game days, when school is not in session, the various Wolves teams divide up and go out to breakfast: the Linemen, the Defensive Secondary, the Offensive Backs and Receivers. Each sub-team finds a place to gather and they eat breakfast.

When they gather around the table, wherever it might be, they take a picture and send it to Coach Gosch. He shares all the pictures and the team is united once again before the game. The pictures tell stories of *play*.

Beyond the traditional *play* activities there are spontaneous pop-up moments of play…bottle flipping wars, races, food eating contests, gym games.

All of these are important investments in the health of the team.

The Wolf Pack is a team. My family is a team. And we deserve to play as well.

One weekend a year—unscheduled and unplanned—we engage in *What If Weekend*. It is a totally fun and goofy idea, but it is a blast and we look forward to it tremendously. In the dead of boring winter, on any given Friday, we each pack one small duffle bag with two sets of clothes and toiletries. We jump in the car and head out. At the first major intersection I ask, "Right or Left?" And one child selects and we turn. The next major intersection, the next child selects right or left and then Mom and Dad take a turn. We continue this until we find a place that looks interesting to stop.

"*What if* we explore here?"

Over the years we have found some amazing places to discover…caves, hiking destinations, great shopping, a spa, a high school baseball field, and a tournament that was so worth watching, a historic village, a beautiful mountain.

Most importantly, each What If Weekend has brought FUN! And so, the objective was met.

The Keeter Center at College of the Ozarks hosts a *Welcome Back* themed party every Fall Semester. Prizes, games, costumes, candies—it has one objective: F. U. N! And the planning is directed by the upper class of students.

Dolly Parton's Stampede in Branson, Missouri, rents out *The Tracks Family Fun Park* once a year so employees can take to the racetracks and compete at will. One objective: F. U. N!

Phoenix Home Care & Hospice hosts a beautiful Christmas Party each year complete with amazing prizes and the infamous *Dance Off* for one simple reason, F. U. N!

The desk-sized ping pong table in the sales manager's office at the *NBC affiliate* in Kansas City is a perfect tool for fun when it's time to think or blow off a little steam.

The ownership of *Harness Roofing, Inc.*, a mid-south commercial roofing business, takes its General Managers and their spouses to a conference in Las Vegas. There are meetings and agenda issues to deal with, but they earmark one day of individualized play for everyone. Each can do just as they please for one free day. For the sole purpose of having fun. It is always interesting to learn that on their free day they choose to hang together and play together. Hmmmm? I wonder why?

General Manager, Bob Hartman, from the *Residence Inn* in Amelia Island, Florida, is a master at gelling a team through the act of play. The team engages in *Bowling Night,* complete with the awful, plastic trophy, the staff *Mannequin Challenge, Spirit Days* where each proudly wear their favorite sporting team jerseys, and periodically, it is *Chef Bob Day* where Bob dons the apron and cooks pancakes, omelets, or lunch for the team. There are too many spontaneous fun activities to name. It all seems to work. This *Residence Inn* ranks in the top 5% of the brand in Guest Satisfaction and has received numerous national brand awards for excellence.

And then there is my own story when I began as the Marketing Manager at the theme park, *Silver Dollar City*, in Branson, Missouri. I learned the value of this lesson by accident. I was a transplant…a *not from around here* immigrant. I was from the city. My history did not cross the paths of any of my team members. The person I was replacing was loved and respected. The team had embraced her, loved her and served her. And, in return, she had loved and served them. I was entering into the culture as the step relative. The tension was not terrible, but the walls were far from thin and transparent. Boundaries were firmly in place.

Now—to add insult to injury, I had set up a photo shoot at the sister water park, sending my Assistant onto location to direct it. And it was a debacle. The photographer had the wrong date. The talent showed up. The Park Leadership had not been informed. And, to make matters worse, it rained. I had been incompetent. I had not done my homework and I sent my Assistant (new relationship) into the fire alone. My Assistant took the butt chewing from the Director of the Water Park.

She arrived back at the office, head down, and shoulders dropped. Walking past my office door without even as much as a glance, she headed to her desk. Anger was echoing from each step. Rightfully so. Another team member stepped forward and told me the tale.

I wanted to apologize—publicly and honestly. It didn't seem enough to call her into my office and have a discussion.

I was dressed in a skirt and suit jacket that day. High heel pumps. Long necklace. I left my desk and entered the hallway; got down on my knees and crawled into our team's office of cubicles. My crawling into the room stopped every eye and every mouth. As I approached her desk we made eye contact.

> "I didn't know any other way to convey how sorry I am for putting you in that position. I know you took the fall. I apologize. I am asking your forgiveness."

Her face stayed solemn at first and then she looked at the runner in my tights sliding down to my ankle and began laughing. She reached into her desk drawer and pulled out a toy Nerf pistol and shot one round of foam bullets at my rear end. Within minutes another employee pulled a toy Nerf gun from her desk. Another tossed me hers and I returned fire. An all-out war broke out. The Vice-President of Marketing appeared from around the corner with a long Nerf rifle and sent everyone under their desks.

In less than thirty minutes the team became one. The Leader was accepted.

All because the act of play leveled the field and broke the tension.

I worked with that team and those relationships for four years. When I left the department to start *Legendary University*, I was presented with a gold-leafed toy Nerf pistol. I still treasure it today.

Is play a part of culture? Yes!

I recently worked with an energy company out of Toronto, Canada. I met the guy in charge of Human Resources for the corporation. But his title wasn't Vice President of Human Resources. It was *Vice President of Culture and People*. I heard him explain, "We are in the people business."

So—what is culture? "The customs, social engagements and achievements of a people." That is one formal definition.

But culture is what makes average turn into amazing. Ordinary to extraordinary. Difficult to easy. Impossible to probable. And boring to fun! Because culture is people—people engaging with people in a way that makes all of us better than one of us.

I read recently that culture is like gravity—pulling, attracting.

During a recent interview with a local business magazine, the journalist asked me a question about retention.

> *"In this rough employment environment where it is so hard to attract and keep good employees, do you have any suggestions?"*

Not to my surprise my mouth started spewing out references to culture and the power of a positive culture to attract employees. Then I ended the interview with a reflection statement.

> *"If you post an open position and the only applicants that appear are the unemployed, the culture of your organization is not a strong one."*

She was taken aback and immediately replied with a request to explain.

> *"If your culture is vibrant, strong, other's-centered and fun, current employees will tell stories about their employer. These will be positive stories. Listeners will hear these stories and reflect on whether or not their own business culture is positive. If it is not—they will sneak on over and apply at the place their friend works. If the only place they learn about your company is in the help wanted sections, there is no story being told. Without a story—there is no strong culture."*

One of the biggest story generating cultural axioms is play.

In a positive culture people play. Just like a pack of wolf pups needs to wrestle to learn what they can and cannot do, boys need to play hog ball when the stakes are low in-order-to understand their potential when the stakes are high, office cultures need to laugh and joke around in-order-to communicate personalities and develop stories of common ground.

Playing not only bonds cultures. It *heals* them.

We smile when we play. We look more human when we smile. And all organizations today can stand for a little more human-ity.

When we play…stories are told. Cultures are marketed.

Now, this seventh lesson of Leadership sounds easy. Far from it. There are some critical points required.

1. The objective of play must be fun.

Dolly Parton's Stampede in Branson is one of three locations for the corporation. My husband, Les Wiest, is the Human Resources Manager. He is atypical for a Human Resources manager, joking with the employees and serving more like a house-mother for a fraternity than a rule instigator. He is guided by one fundamental difference in the world of Human Resources: He believes that most HR departments focus on rules…"don't break these policies and procedures and you won't get fired." But his mantra is different: "Do these things and you will be successful." He is truly an *internal marketer*, consistently marketing *Dolly Parton's Stampede Branson* as a preferred place to work… *"the most fun place to work!"*

So, when the kitchen received a new piece of equipment one day and it came in a huge refrigerator-sized box, Les didn't see a piece of cardboard that needed to go to recycling. He saw an opportunity for play.

The Director of Operations hid inside of the box and they cut two arm holes in the side. Les had to call employees into his office one morning for benefits open enrollment. Inside the box was the Director of Ops waiting for the unsuspecting employee to arrive. At just the right moment he would reach his arms out of the box for a grand surprise. Screams and howls filled the hallways. Laughter roared. Play happened.

And the Branson location enjoys the lowest turnover of any of the company locations.

2. Fun is defined by those you serve—not you.

Before Phil and Kimberly Melugin launched *Phoenix Home Care* and Hospice, Phil stood at the Captain's wheel of the launch of another home health care agency that began in Kansas City, expanded to Springfield, Missouri, and created a successful path throughout the Midwest. After 10+ years of effective Leadership, a hostile takeover by the other partners interrupted the path, and Phil and Kimberly found themselves launching the *Phoenix* vision from that pile of ashes.

During Phil's reign at the helm, the company had a regionally-famous Christmas party. Stories were shared all year long about the party. Associates carved the date in stone on their calendars. Dresses and suits were bought months in advance. Everyone attended. The party planning committee always included a mixture of associates from all levels. Leadership served the associates with this party. It was for them, about them, developed by them, and paid for by the company. The beloved local rock and blues band was their choice as was the food, the prizes, and the activities.

Phil had to stand up to his partners every year to keep the party associate-centered. Their desire was to put more messaging into the party, have a state-of-the-union-style keynote address with a big dose of ministry, select the prizes that would spawn personal development and life enrichment, and…provide the entertainment themselves as singers.

One of the first things that changed, after Phil's departure, was the Christmas party. For two years the party continued but it was directed by Ownership. An owner's wife bought all the prizes which were mainly home decorating arrangements from her network of resources. There was a lengthy speech with directive content, and performance singing. The attendance the first year was high. The second year it dwindled. In the third year the event was terminated due to, what the Associates heard as, *"inexplicable lack of interest and attitude problems."*

The death of the Christmas party was not due to the attitudes of the pack, but rather was driven by myopic leaders who had grown out of touch with their team.

After setting growth records for the first 11 years of the company's life, it has only grown a total of 11% in the past 7 years.

I remember a broadcasting boss I had once that loved basketball. It was truly his passion. It made sense when Corporate told him to make sure we had some down days; when our sales team hit its goals, we should do something fun.

So, every single time we hit our sales goals, we played basketball. And there were many on our team that hated basketball. But our Boss would show up on playday with the terrycloth absorbent head band and the high-top shoes. He would ask people to accept his bet that he could dunk the basketball and we would all throw a buck in and watch him dunk. He would call out the two teams, with his being comprised of the better athletes…and we would play basketball.

We hated it.

But this same point carries over into the next point.

3. Successful play is bottom up.
It's not about the Leader.

After each of us had fulfilled the obligatory basketball game of fun for the Boss, we would bid him farewell and rendezvous at a neighborhood bar without him. And that is where the fun happened. We played table shuffleboard, drank beer, and laughed about how much we sucked at basketball and how silly the Boss looked in his headband.

The easy way to adhere to this rule for organized play is to ask, "How do you guys want to celebrate together?" And then if no one has great ideas, offer up a few and take a vote. It is about the team…not the Leader.

4. The best play is not scheduled.

Close your eyes and imagine Hitler in a suit and tie stating (just before he demands the trademark heel clap), "Vi vill have fun!"

There are Leaders who believe fun during scheduled playtime can be mandated. If play time is mandated it must be called *team building*, which can also be fun but it is a whole different concept with a different objective.

The spontaneous Nerf war in my office was fun because it was a pop-up war. Imagine how weak that would have been if I'd walked in and handed everyone a Nerf gun and said, *"Now it is time to shoot each other."*

When the Wolves Coaches show up with water balloons, let the players just horse around, wheel out a cooler of ice pops on a hot day, turn the sprinklers on unannounced, encourage a spontaneous bottle-flipping contest, or just let a game of touch football break out…it is fun and unscheduled.

5. Sometimes we just need *Permission to Play*.

The Leader's job is to create a culture where play is, not only allowed, but expected and encouraged.

There is a wonderful hotel in Boston. It is *The Courtyard by Marriott at Copley Square*. The General Manager is a delightful leader named Bernardo Gubert. He understands the power of play, not only for his team members, but for his guests.

When a guest checks into the hotel and enters their assigned room, he or she finds a stuffed toy sheep sitting on the bed. The sheep is named Exeter (after the famed address of the hotel's 100-year-old building—88 Exeter Street). Exeter holds a card explaining that he is a wonderful reminder to count sheep and sleep well. But he also explains that he gets bored sitting in the room and he wants to do more than just jump around in people's dreams. He wants to play.

Exeter encourages guests to take him with them on their travels around Boston, take pictures with him, post those pictures on social media, and compete for prizes and rewards for playing. Bernardo's team then selects pictures daily and awards getaways, dinners, prizes, and hilarious comments. It is all wonderful fun. The story of the hotel is shared. And guests have their own story to tell.

The ironic thing is Exeter is also for sale if you want to take him home. And quite frequently, Exeter finds his way into the suitcase. Why?

People like to play. Sometimes they just need a permission slip—or sheep—that lets them know it is expected and encouraged.

Schedule recess. Surprise someone with cookies or a lunch. Let everyone make an ice cream run or schedule the ice cream truck to make a surprise stop at the office. Have a water balloon fight. Have a picnic. Or—if the whole office loves basketball, play ball!

Remember the only rule of play is **F. U. N**!

F = FORGET about all other objectives…it's just playing. Let it go!
U = UNITE your team members together…everyone has the opportunity to play.
N = It's NOT about you—ever!

APPLICATION

1. Look at your culture. Is it tired, stressed, bored? If so…rock the boat with some play time. Start small. Food is always a good way to start. One day just bring in a fun food. Something as simple as donuts can work. Be present in the room with the donuts and relax, joke, chat, and eat a donut. Don't control conversation or encourage people to get back to work. Just let it go for a little while. Let it be. Then—when you are alone, back in your office, think about what you experienced, and what you learned.

2. Find an outside affiliation—something that can emotionally connect with people on your team…such as a charity walk, a basketball challenge, a bike outing…Let your team decide. Simply let them know you would like to do something as a *team* that would help another organization or charity that people are passionate about. Let them pick and then just be a participant. Don't lead the event. Don't manage it. Let it go.

3. Locate one of those silly national calendars that feature special days—such as *National Ice Cream Day, National Bright Sock Day, National Pajama Day, National Bring Your Dog To Work Day*. Find a national day or two around which your team could rally. Let it happen—just give permission to play.

4. Take an employee to lunch about once every two weeks or so. Ask him or her how they think the team could have more fun at work. Pick brains, get ideas, give away the right to think up fun things. Encourage others to own it. Let them become in charge of fun.

5. Never let a birthday or work anniversary go by without doing something that is fun for the honoree.

LESSON EIGHT

Celebrate

Wolf Trait

Noses touch. Tails and butts wag. Howls fill the sky. It is time to celebrate. A big kill has happened. A filling meal has been consumed. The pack is healthy for another day.

Wolves nuzzle each other and growl low, contented growls. A creative mind may even witness a smile. Social animals praise one another and celebrate. But they do not celebrate the performance…they celebrate the pack. They are not high-fiving the wolf who delivered the killing bite. They celebrate the whole pack. Very important point in the wolf pack. They celebrate, not to repeat the performance, but to honor the successful coming together of the pack. Evolution has developed our brains to recognize the power, safety, and improved quality of life by being a part of the whole. Social species such as wolves thrive being a part of a bigger whole and they express that in the form of joyful celebration.

I couldn't believe it. I said it was possible. But I honestly didn't know if I believed my own words. One year earlier in the Conference Title match-up, when Adam yelled "What the hell?" with such honest passion, I knew the Wolves could have beaten the monster big school. I knew it was just a few missed opportunities that caused the loss. But I wasn't sure I really believed all that! It had not been done by anyone in 65 conference games. No one had beaten this team. Our Wolves had never beaten them since the monster had grown into a 4A-sized school. It had been 13 years since the Wolves claimed victory over this nemesis and even then, the monster was a smaller, rural school.

But on this night…On our beautiful home field…The Wolves won! And the Conference Title would forever carry our name.

My husband and I ran to the field with the hundreds of other parents and fans. Coach Gosch stood at center field on the iconic wolf. Every boy took a knee around him and he spoke.

His words were fast, passionate and strong!

"Now *that* is accountability!"

"*That* is playing for the guy next to you!"

"You all won! Every one of you!"

"You *are* a *team*!"

Isn't it amazing that he wasn't celebrating just the win? He was celebrating the *mission*. He was celebrating all that they had talked about all year.

Then…this contained, controlled, strong, ever-focused Coach began to do something no one had ever seen. *He danced*. He jumped so high his feet topped the heads of the kneeling players. He laughed. He squealed and joyful tears leapt from his eyes.

He celebrated with all his heart!

The finish line was successfully crossed and the whole world was right and complete in that moment.

And it was time to celebrate.

It is easy to wrap our minds and memories around celebrating a victory in sports. We have all experienced some element of that. But it gets a little harder to find those definable moments in business. Here are a few really important points.

Yes, Coach Gosch celebrated the victory. But his words were about *team* and *attitude* and Tiny Focus. He praised each player for giving his all. He praised the team. He praised Alignment—Assignment. He praised having the belief that it was possible. In other words, he celebrated *becoming better men.*

He connected the celebration to the Vision and Mission.

If you are raising better men, celebrate players behaving like better men.

What you celebrate, what you reward, will get done.

Pull up positive behavior and you will get more of that behavior.

Taking time to celebrate is not something that readily happens in the workplace. I remember at *Silver Dollar City* I often became very tired of not being able to find finish lines. There was always another goal to achieve. No official breaks create a very tired team. It is the Leader's role to make breaks, to create finish lines and to pause for celebration.

Celebrate progress—not perfection of total achievement.

> Celebration is a necessary stop along the leadership continuum. And it is the Leader's responsibility.

Coach Gosch would say after every Friday night victory, "Enjoy this win. Wrap up in it over the weekend. Come back Monday ready to work again."

We all need to wrap up in celebration at times.

Finish lines are necessary.

Knowing there will be an end and a time to celebrate keeps us journeying forward. Without knowing the finish line, we can imagine the mirage and be very disheartened at the monotony of it all. The tasks become the wheel in the hamster cage and we just run to nowhere.

Celebration feeds the human need to truly know we are making a significant difference. Each of us honestly wants to make a positive difference. It makes us feel good. Research after research shows that the feeling of making a positive difference is a top reason for continued employment with any organization. The leader must take time to confirm that positive difference.

Celebration gives us the opportunity to talk about the positive difference someone is making in this world.

For instance:

> "Mary—your name was mentioned on a TripAdvisor comment because you helped a little boy find his lost teddy bear in our hotel. It touched his mother's heart so much that she took time to write about it and it posted to thousands of readers. Great job, Mary. You are helping us all be so very successful."

> "Frank—Hitting your sales goals this month is amazing. Not only will you receive your bonus for the month, but because of your contribution, we are able to hire another person in the phone room to help with the overflow."

> Celebration of impactful behaviors confirms the positive difference people are making in this world.

And making a positive difference matters!

It is a critical employee retention best practice.

As Leaders in business, we have no problem understanding external marketing. We put our promises and key appeals on billboards, in social media, on brochures. We spend millions on radio and television ads. We tell the world about what makes us different and why he or she should use our product or service. When a customer does business with us a lot we reward them for that behavior. We give them reward points. We punch frequent shopper cards. We offer special spending cash for a return visit. We put them on the MPC list—*Most Profitable Customer*. We treat them like gold.

Other customers see this happening and they want to experience the same treatment. In the airport, the *Gold Medallion* passengers get to walk down the red carpet to board the plane before anyone else. And those of us in Zone 2 stand in awe and jealously at their coolness. Next time we book a flight we remember and think about building loyalty with that airline so someday we might see *Priority* on our boarding pass!

All of that is easy to grasp in external marketing. We can and should take that same mindset *inside* of our organizations for *internal marketing*. We should know what we want our team members to do and then develop rewards and recognition when they do it. Keep that stage illuminated with spotlights so they will continue to climb up on it.

Meyer Jabara Hotels Mirrors Celebrations; Phoenix Home Care and Hospice Rise Above For Excellence Quarterly Awards; Legendary Memory Maker Awards at *Herschend Family Entertainment*; Iron Wolf stickers on helmets...

Loyalty of mission driven behavior by employees is as important or more important than celebrating the loyal behavior of the external customer.

Why?

Because the customer experience can never rise higher on the experience continuum than the experience and attitude of the employee. The employee carries the key to a successful customer experience in their hands—not in the hands of Leadership. High tide raises all boats and low tide grounds them.

Celebrate your internal customer's behaviors.
Internally market them. Create a loyalty program.

It is critically important for the Leader to celebrate and to shine the light on the stage of significance, but the Leader cannot see all and be all. Sometimes it is even more meaningful when the Leader passes the baton and lets others seek the positive behavior.

One of the most influential and visionary Leaders I know is Mary Kellogg-Joslyn from the *Titanic Museum Attraction*. I am proud and honored to call her friend.

Mary is Executive Vice President and co-owner of *Cedar Bay Entertainment*, which brings to life the *Titanic Museum Attraction* experiences in Branson, Missouri, and Pigeon Forge, Tennessee. She is the leader of developing and coordinating marketing, advertising, operations, sales, merchandising, public relations, and all things Titanic. I believe her biggest strength is ensuring everyone on her team has the training and skills to perform their jobs at excellence.

Pre-launch of the *Titanic* experience, Mary served as Executive Vice President of Television for *The Walt Disney Company*. She brought the highly successful *Live! With Regis and Kathie Lee* show into the homes of millions. She helped create, develop, and deliver *Who Wants to Be a Millionaire* plus many other weekly and daily productions.

The *Titanic Museum Attraction* is a labor of love and true passion for both Mary and her husband, John Joslyn who, in 1987, co-led the 6-million-dollar expedition to the site of the sinking. The team's mission was to explore the wreckage, and film the broken remains. 44 days and 32 dives later, there was enough footage for John Joslyn and his partner, Doug Lewelyn, to produce *Return to Titanic…Live!*, a two-hour television special that became the second highest rated live TV documentary in history.

The attractions in both Missouri and Tennessee are *RMS Titanic*-shaped structures built in tribute to the 2,208 passengers and crew who were on board in 1912 when she sailed her fateful voyage. The mission of the *Titanic* team is to keep the passengers' and crews' memories alive by simply telling their stories every day.

It is an incredible experience. Uniformed crew members seamlessly carry the guests through an engaging experience of exploration and delight. Children's eyes dance as they climb atop ship decks that begin to slant—slightly at the beginning when the ship first hit the iceberg, then gradually discovering how impossible it was to hang on as the decks assumed the 90-degree angle.

Ladies gaze at the beautiful china served in the First-Class dining room and imagine days of elegance and grace.

Little boys and big men run their hands along the polished wood of the ship's wheel and call out "Iceberg!" into the dark, cold night.

Little girls stand with eyes wide open staring at the beautiful ball gowns and glistening shoes…dreaming of the princesses that climbed the grand staircase.

Moment after moment one can spy couples joining hands as they climb the Grand Staircase. A return to the days of sophisticated, welcomed chivalry, and romance.

It is two or more hours of unforgettable hands-on history.

To create this kind of experience day in and day out requires incredible leadership. The cast and crew members need to know that each engagement is important and all decisions made impact the treasured memories of the guests.

Mary Kellogg and Vice President Danita Brown cannot possibly be in two ships every day for each guest engagement. The task—and honor—of finding positive behavior must be placed in more hands.

Enter Back Stage Magic.

What is Back Stage Magic?

This is a monthly crew recognition program that rewards members for having performed kind-spirited services outside of their assigned work area. Crew members themselves submit names of fellow crew mates whom they feel deserve special recognition for extra good-deed performances. The peers pull up peers.

Managers then identify three crew members in the selected group to be acknowledged and rewarded for their random acts of kindness.

> "Our Mission Statement is to honor and celebrate Titanic passengers' lives. Our Back Stage Magic concept has similar goals—to honor and celebrate the special lives and achievements of our exceptional crew." -Mary Kellogg

Crew Members include those in Admissions, Maintenance, Retail, Phone Reservations, Sales, Receiving, Accounting, IT, Data Entry, and

Receptionist. It is a way to honor those behind the scenes that make it all possible.

The names are submitted by peers. Peers catching peers doing the exceptional mission-driven work.

Then the recognition is also significantly important.

Each person who nominated the winning individuals as well as the managers, often the Vice President, and even Mary Kellogg, show up for Backstage Magic awards. It is a public presentation where stories are shared. Significance and purpose are so prominent, everyone understands why the awards are given. Prizes vary. If something special is in town the prizes might be tickets to an event. Sometimes gift cards, food gift certificates, shopping or gas cards. It is always a thoughtful award.

Today the world is quick. Birthday greetings are sent automatically by software programs with electronic signatures. One can even hit the party hat icon on Facebook and complete the task of telling a friend it is time to celebrate. Email and text, instant messaging, and social media have taken the difficulty out of sending well wishes and congratulations.

But something has been lost along the way. Effort and often sincerity are shallow. Now I am not an old prude. I know the social media stage is a big one and a well-written thank you personally sent or publicly posted can mean a lot. It can even *market* the behaviors of one to thousands.

But sometimes a personal note, handwritten and delivered in person can mean the world.

Each year Mary Kellogg designs a *Titanic* birthday card. It is truly a special design. It is only for the cast and crew of the ships. Every team member receives one from the owners, Mary Kellogg and John Joselyn, on his or her birthday. There is a handwritten note inside with a personal comment and a wish. One of the longtime crew members shared with me a file containing every card. "Oh—these are worth keeping," she declared. "I even have one colleague who turned them into a wall collage. They are so beautiful and mean so much."

Back Stage Magic is special, not only because it is peers celebrating peers, but because it is done on a stage and for that moment the recipient is a star.

The Mirrors Celebration I wrote about earlier from the *Meyer Jabara Hotels Company* is special not only because of peer-to-peer nomination and selection but because the ceremony is hosted by the owners, in front of leadership and peers, and the invited guests of honor may bring a person of significance from their own lives with them.

1. Sending an email or text thanking an associate for good work is *fine*. But fine is the cop-out to *great*.

2. Writing a handwritten note and mailing it…or having an assistant type it up, signing it and mailing it is a little better. It takes a little more effort.

3. Writing that note and delivering to the associate in person; shaking their hand and saying, "thank you" is better.

4. Writing that note, delivering it, shaking that hand and doing it publicly in front of peers is even better.

5. Writing that note, delivering it, shaking that hand, doing it publicly in front of peers *and* thanking someone of significance in their personal life for sharing this special person with the team is amazing!

Celebration is not an after-thought. It is not something Leaders do when they have time. It is a necessary, purposeful, intentional act of Leadership that has true impact in the lives of the people we serve and in our own success.

Celebrate heart.

We want good guys to finish first sometimes. It is always tough to see the less than character-based people get ahead in the world. We ache to believe in the goodness of man. We want heroes. We crave to vote for someone instead of just against another. We really want the good guy to get ahead too. It's tough when the starter is also the trash talker in the locker room and the guy that makes fun of teammates. That starter might be extremely talented, and we love his or her skill. We need their skill. But we want the guy that offers a hand up when you fall, that shows up early, that offers to help when it's closing time and your stack of to do items is still sky high. We want to celebrate the guy that keeps a secret and protects the back of his teammates.

Just ask how much money the movie *Rudy* has made. Everybody wants a Rudy to cheer for and that moment of deserved recognition fulfilled.

Need is strong. Need makes tough decisions. But want is a passionate quest…a driver…a gravitational force. I would much rather have my husband *want* me than *need* me.

Skill and natural ability are awarded with points on the scoreboard and cheers from the stands. It is up to the Leader to convey that *heart* matters too.

That is why it is always important to let peers honor peers. The peers know the truth. Politics go out the window when the front line is asked to tell the story.

> Great Leaders celebrate the good guy, too.

> Celebrate heart and other hearts will follow.

A coveted award among the Football Wolves is the *Iron Wolf Award*. It is given to one player per grade on which the team can count. It is the guy that always shows up, always gives 110%, always speaks positively, and stands for the pack. The *Iron Wolf* recipient carries the heart of the Wolves with him always and does whatever it takes to find a way.

This award is given every year at the end of year awards celebration. Our first year as high school parents we sat in the room and listened to the description of the award. Tears filled my eyes as I thought about the dedication of this individual and the character.

Then, when the name was read, I blanked on what else was said. It was the name of our son. It was the most incredible character honor I could imagine. In that moment he became, *Forever a Wolf*.

Celebration and honoring character matters. If you want more character-based behavior on your team—celebrate it—honor it—reward it.

🐾 🐾 🐾

The *Wing Man Award* at *Phoenix Home Care and Hospice* is named appropriately. The Wing Man does not lead or draw attention or search the spotlight. The Wing Man has the other guy's wing at all times.

I've Got Your Back!

It is the pinnacle award in the *Taking Flight* culture. It is treasured and when the recipient's name is announced at the annual Christmas Party, the room erupts with applause, gasps of joy and a standing ovation. Why? Because we *want* the good guy to win and ride the white horse across the stage.

You are the Leader. When the world witnesses you celebrating those that are getting closer to the compelling vision that you casted oh so long ago, they understand the process.

And the circle of the Iron Wolf Journey begins again!

People will stand in line to be a part of it all.

APPLICATION

1. Read your Mission Statement. Identify the behaviors necessary to bring that mission to life. Figure out a way to recognize when those behaviors happen and then make time to celebrate or pull up those behaviors.

2. Create a peer-to-peer recognition opportunity and make a big deal about it.

3. Find mini-goals that you can market as milestones. Publish those goals and celebrate goal attainment along the way to the big goals of the quarter or the year.

4. Publicly thank the good guy every now and then…for living the mission.

It was over. The season was complete. It ended in a loss.

For every team, except for one in each district, there is an end just short of the State Title. And so, it was for our Wolves. But we had gone further than any team ever had. We were Conference Champs!

We joined the other parents and fans on the field. Our son walked toward us. His eyes met mine. His tears flowed freely. The tears were sad. But they were also a release. So much work had gone into those tears…months and months of weight training, conditioning, hitting, working hard. As a Freshman, he had been privileged to become part of the Varsity team. As a Sophomore, he found his moments of contribution and the chance to earn a letter that outwardly showed his belonging. As a Junior, he earned his spot and protected it with every ounce of his being. He played for the guy next to him. He was a part of The Pack. His heart was breaking that it was over. The Senior Wolves would never be on the field with him again.

"I'm going to miss 'em, Mom." He was talking about the Seniors. "I can't believe we're done."

What makes a teenage boy sorry that he doesn't have to work two and a half hours longer each school day? What makes him sad that he doesn't have to get hit by 250+ pound Senior Lineman anymore? What makes him tear up over not having to run sprints until his muscles just can't go one more step?

The answer…being a part of something bigger than himself.

> *Team. Vision. Accountability. Respect. Contribution. Learning. Accomplishment. Brotherhood. Fun.*

When you live inside of a positive culture,

> work toward a compelling vision,
>
> become a part of something bigger than oneself,
>
> leave your mark,
>
> learn and grow,
>
> share your ideas,
>
> make the world a better place,
>
> have fun together,

and celebrate…

It is sad when it is over!

Connor's Junior year ended with an amazing winning record and another Conference Title. The final game was the second round of District Competition and the final score was extremely close. It was a well-fought game, well-played. Two skilled teams working the clock. And we came up short.

The final huddle formed and one Senior stood. He bowed his head and began to pray. He thanked the Father for the opportunity to play the game. He didn't mention the loss. He mentioned the gift of brotherhood and he quoted First Corinthians.

"Love bears all things, believes all things, hopes all things, endures all things."

After the *amen*, he raised his head. With tears streaming down his cheeks he proclaimed, *"I love you guys. You are forever my brothers."*

One by one the young men stood up. Each began to hug the other.

"I love you."
"I will always remember you guys."
"I love you."
"I'll never forget."
"Brothers forever."

It is love. It is true love. It is the love of brotherhood. It is the altruistic love of team. Being a part of something bigger than oneself means that we love something bigger than oneself. It is passion. It is something our world needs more of.

A few days passed after the final game. I was at a luncheon and a woman who had witnessed the game asked me a question. Its source was a place of naiveté. I felt sad for her. She honestly didn't know the answer to her question. Her heart did not know the answer.

She asked, "Why on earth would a guy cry after losing a football game?"

The inexperienced mind answers with obvious replies:

"Because we were undefeated."

"Because it was for the championship."

"Because we came so close but didn't get it done."

But there is a better answer that finds its source in the heart:

"Because he loves."

If I owned a company that cared about its product—that wanted to create memories for the customers it served—that wanted to build brand loyalty—that wanted to change the world...I would hire the one that cried.

A culture of passionate excellence will always win.

The definition of win doesn't mean the final score of a game.

It is bigger than that.

Winning means learning for self, deepening relationships with others and making the world a better place no matter how big or small.

Through the eyes of this customer-parent...the Coach achieved the vision. Better men are rising.

THE STATE OF PERPETUAL LEADERSHIP

The Seniors graduated. It was the best year in Reeds Spring Football history. Many went on to play football in college.

The park bench analysts said the loss of the key Seniors would be felt dramatically. It would have to be a re-building year.

What they didn't understand was the power of The Pack. The pack is organic, ever-changing, and self-preserving. It adapts to survive. Those that once lived in the shadows of the stronger and older now rise to the occasion and fill the holes. New leaders emerge. It is the wolf way.

Are you an Iron Wolf Leader?

Can you take individuals and create a PACK?

When you follow the Eight Lessons, W.O.L.F. Leadership becomes alive and drives success.

What is Iron W.O.L.F. Leadership?

Whole Vision

Have you ever tried to put a jigsaw puzzle together? The first thing I do is grab the box and look at the finished picture. Then I look at the pieces that have the flat edges and start to create the borders or playing field. Next, I put all the like colors together and begin to place those colors into piles where I think they go in relation to the whole picture.

Leaders must make sure all those that are doing the doing know what the whole picture is going to look like when we are done. Great Coaches help players visualize and actually feel what it would be like to win. Great Business Leaders explain the goal and how it contributes to the mission and the vision.

Ownership of Outcomes

Put the power closest to the doing. Give people the gift of ownership so they think, process, and act. When the person closest to the ball makes a choice based on all the current realities and takes actions, progress is made in the moment. If he must stop and ask the Coach what to do, the other team has already scored!

If the customer needs something, the person closest to that customer needs to take action in the moment, or else the customer will move on to someone who can serve her more quickly and relate to her.

Learn as You Go

The classroom is a great place to learn, but life is even a better learning partner. Having the mindset of learning and applying that learning produces constant improvement.

Why do the Wolves watch game film? Not to see how well they did, but rather to see what they *did*, looking for behaviors, application of learning, and improvement.

What did we do? What did we learn? How do we get better by applying what we learned?

Pass it on!

Feed the Success of Others

Our son, Connor, is now a Senior. The final summer of his weight training is beginning. But there is something different this year. His little brother, Caden, is entering seventh grade. He is eligible for Monday through Thursday weight training and conditioning. This eavesdropping mother heard a conversation coming from the basement that touched my heart.

"Wow…I just saw the calendar for summer. It looks like I have to go four days a week to work out! That's a bummer!" Caden said with angst in his voice.

"Really? Check yourself! You don't *have to* go four days a week. You *get to* go four days a week. That's a privilege."

Feed the success of others! Grow others by coaching the mindset. Set the expectation. Touch the heart. Character over skill every time.

We deserve to be promoted and stand on the stage of acknowledgement as a Great Leader, not when we do our work well, but when we have grown others to do our work well.

Wolves roam. Alphas come and go. Some are beaten and run away. Some graduate and go on to spread the learning. Pups are born and rise up to lead. Omegas learn or leave. The one constant is the PACK. Let there always be a pack and a passionate howling band of leaders who make the journey worth taking.

AN AFTERTHOUGHT

Sitting in the stands of the last football game of the season I realize—I am just a mom.

But as I close out my introspection of watching my son grow through the game of football at the hands of great leadership, I have never been prouder. And there is no greater position on earth than that of a parent in support of his or her child growing into a responsible, contributing adult. When he understands that he is a part of something bigger than himself, we have all succeeded.

I close my eyes and my children are little again. Their feet fit in the palm of my hand. Their scratches and scrapes are fixed with kisses. Their tears are diminished with ice cream cones and summer walks in the woods. But when I open my eyes I see men…Because of each day spent driving to practices—working through the disappointment and the challenges—scrubbing grass stains out of pants—discovering the meaning of *high protein*—breathing deeply—building self-confidence—cheering passionately—biting tongues—and supporting Coaches who we must believe love them…they are men.

We have all succeeded. And the world is a better place.

Football is a great game. It teaches the power of brotherhood, of team, of finding a way through adversity. It teaches so many life lessons, but it requires the heart of a learner and the skill of a Leader.

Life is a great game. We must lead with the power of *brotherhood* and s*isterhood*, of team, of finding a way through adversity, of winning.

Great Leadership makes all things possible in any pack.

Find your Pack.

Connor

Caden

Through His Eyes

"To me, being a member of The Pack means that no matter what, someone has my back. Whether I'm struggling in class or I'm struggling with a relationship, I know that someone else has been through the same thing as me and he cares. We all put in blood, sweat, and tears to be in The Pack and we have developed a special bond through that. There's no better feeling than being backed by your brothers. Brothers forever." -Connor Wiest, our son.

EPILOGUE

Fast forward to today. I stand in my driveway as Connor, now a Sophomore in college, drives his younger brother, Caden, to the high school where a self-formed group of boys are going to *play a little game or two*. No Coaches are present. Kids are tired of sitting around. Spring Break has been extended due to COVID-19. The virus hasn't spread to our part of the world yet, but the schools and restaurants are closed. What started as a group text ended up as a vicious game of two-hand touch. Two-hand touch grew into racing for the fastest 40. The competition ended with a field goal kick-off. As I arrived two hours later to pick up Caden, I saw the young men resting on the turf…just talking, connecting, and dreaming. The lights will turn on again. The ball will find the air again. The talk will heat up and the sweat will pour again.

It is the way it is in The Pack. It is the way it will always be.

Coach Gosch has turned the page to a new chapter, accepting the role of Athletic Director for the Wolves. There is a new guy in town, a 15-year high school football coach named Andy McFarland. His record tells a story of winning championships.

> "Once a culture is established, the smart guy meets it where it is and carries it to where it can grow. Winning teams share common characteristics. Winning is a habit. So is losing. This culture will be a solid foundation to build the habit of winning."

A huge question rests in the minds of all who care.

> *"Can a new leader protect, perpetuate, and progress the culture?"*

The answer is a definite "yes" if he is driven by Core Values. When the new Leader understands that the culture, well led, is stronger than any playbook or individual athlete, he will thrive and so will the culture.

The howl begins. The voice is different, but the message is the same.

Integrity

Consistency

Enthusiasm

Grit

Fun

Hard Work

Pack!

And the howl is answered.

SUMMARY OF THE EIGHT LESSONS

LESSON ONE: CAST A COMPELLING VISION

1. A great leader casts a *compelling* vision. It is not a boring and safe vision. It is beautiful, lofty, and challenging.

2. If he/she wants and needs others to journey toward that vision too, he/she does not write that vision alone.

3. Those that journey must see themselves in that vision and understand how they contribute to bringing it into view.

4. The vision must have behaviors attached to it. Answering the question, "What are the expectations and rules of the journey?"

5. The vision is best conveyed through storytelling and word pictures.

6. The story must be told often and celebrated.

7. The vision rules. We do not lower the brightness and the beauty of the vision just to make us feel better and more comfortable.

LESSON TWO: PACK

1. Culture exists with or without leadership. But to enable a culture to achieve goals, that culture must be led purposefully and intentionally.

2. Culture is powerful. The culture of the pack will make or break any strategy created.

3. Each member of the pack must know the role they play in the success equation and see himself or herself marching in the celebration parade. In other words, each knows his contribution and feels necessary on the journey toward goal attainment.

4. Each member of the pack must know how the guy next to him on the team needs him and therefor feels a sense of belonging and responsibility.

5. Leaders model accountability and allow peers to hold peers accountable. Accountability is not about blame. It is about ownership. It is about love. We know what greatness feels like and we want those we lead to feel it too. We care enough to hold them accountable.

6. Iron sharpens iron. Let the best and the brightest lead and challenge. Greatness begets greatness.

7. The best pack always wins—no matter what the competition.

LESSON THREE: ENCOURAGE TRACKS

1. Individual empowerment fully inculcated into a culture is necessary for excellent team performance.

2. Empowerment is not a buzzword. There are key components necessary to have a culture of empowered team members fulfilling the mission one decision at a time.

a. A well-defined playing field.

b. Training on skill sets required to take idyllic actions.

c. Coaching based on performance so learning can be applied.

d. Celebration of appropriate actions that balance the results for all stakeholders.

3. Leading isn't about the Leader. The Leader isn't always present. Individual members of the pack need to know how

they contribute and be willing to make decisions and take actions on their own—for the good of the whole.

4. The individual records and praise come not by striving for individual fame but rather by working for the guy next to you. When we do what is best for the mission, we find that we are recognized as a great individual performer as well.

5. Leaders leave footprints for all to see. We must make sure they are ones of which we are proud.

LESSON FOUR: LEARN

1. Leaders (Coaches) must help others see the elements (ingredients) of success. The magic is in the moments.

2. It is impossible to manage whole days, experiences or chunks of time. Great Leaders know the power of Tiny Focus.

3. We train ourselves to examine steps that must be in place *at excellence* so we can achieve our desired outcome. Then when we fall off that level of excellence we don't get upset with the whole machine. We examine the broken part.

4. It takes a process to ensure we manage moments and lead the people to own those moments.

5. Through it all, the most important cultural must do is capture learning and apply the intelligence gathered.

6. Great leaders create cultures filled with learners hungry to engage in learning opportunities. Seekers of learning are valuable to the team.

7. Sometimes our greatest teachers don't carry the official title of *Director—Boss—Trainer*. Always we learn by looking through the eyes of those we serve.

LESSON FIVE: COMMUNICATE

1. We can never be perfect at communication. Communication is like air. You take a breath and then you

just want another one. Those we lead will always want, need and ask for more communication.

2. Successful communication is when the information is received and understood in the manner it was intended and those involved have had an opportunity to speak into it.

3. Communication is not dropping information into a black hole. We need to know how it was received and if the desired behaviors as a result of it are understood. It is like sitting in the exit row of an airplane. When the flight attendant asks you if you understand the obligations of sitting in that row you must acknowledge with a verbal "Yes!"

4. We need formal and informal communication. We must be intentional about both.

5. If all we share is "need to know" information, the culture will fill in the rest. That's called gossip.

6. Sharing "want to know" and "nice to know" information is a great employee retention strategy and drives culture.

7. Communication is not sharing information; it is having conversations.

LESSON SIX: SERVE OTHERS

1. Effective Leaders find their greatest joy in the accomplishment and recognition of those they lead.

2. It feels good to be a part of something bigger than self and to serve a greater good. We must help those we lead find their service purpose.

3. We must lose the *in order to* so as to serve and benefit from the pure joy of serving and positive results serving produces.

4. We best serve with an *Outside In* approach. We look at those we serve and identify with them what *Great Performance* looks like. And then we help them get there. That is *others-centered service vs. self-centered service*.

5. We must align our actions to the greater goal—not just our siloed, personal goals. *Alignment—Assignment.* Only then do we serve the better team.

6. Helping others see what they cannot see from their current position is a great leadership role...*and* it keeps us *wanted* at the table.

LESSON SEVEN: PLAY

1. Play is a critical objective for every successful team.

2. Play that produces the outcome of *fun* develops bonds, infuses fresh ideas, reduces tension, and creates stories.

3. Stories of fun and brotherhood/sisterhood market culture. And when we market culture we have an easier time recruiting and retaining.

4. Recap:

a. The objective of play must be fun—nothing else.

b. Fun is defined by those you serve—not you.

c. Successful play is not about the Leader.

d. Play shouldn't be scheduled—just made time for.

e. Give permission to play. *Celebrate play.*

LESSON EIGHT: CELEBRATE

1. *Celebration is not an afterthought.* It's a really important big deal.

2. What we celebrate will be cloned.

3. We need finish lines or milestones when the vision or destination is just too far away to see.

4. Celebrate mission-driven behaviors, not just goal attainment.

5. Use celebration as an internal marketing tool to spotlight what is important to you and to the team.

6. Remember to celebrate the good guy, too.

ABOUT THE AUTHOR

Terri is a professional speaker, facilitator, writer, and leadership consultant. She has owned and operated Tucker Resources since 1996 and serves clients worldwide in many industries.

Terri has a gift of helping others look through the eyes of those they serve and find opportunities for growth. She coaches leadership to help develop practices, messages, and offerings that differentiate and drive success. Facilitation of strategic plans, annual goals, Mission, Vision, and Value Statements is also a proven practice for Terri.

Keynote addresses and entertaining presentations are among Terri's strongest offerings.

Terri has a rich marketing background, having served as Marketing Director for KMBC-TV; Hearst Broadcasting. and KYTV; Schurz Communications. She was Marketing Director for Silver Dollar City…a Herschend Family Entertainment Property. (Herschend Family Entertainment owns properties such as Stone Mountain Park in Georgia, Silver Dollar City in Branson, Missouri, and Dollywood in Tennessee.)

She is the creator and founder of Herschend Family Entertainment's corporate training center, Legendary University…an internal marketing and leadership training retreat.

Terri has most recently launched PHC University, the corporate training center for Phoenix Home Care and Hospice—Missouri, Colorado, Kansas, and Illinois. This leadership training academy prepares leaders of the organization to achieve high performance.

Terri is an understudy of the renowned author and coach, Dr. James Belasco, most noted for his best-selling leadership guide *Flight of the Buffalo*. Terri brings the foundational principles and tools taught in *Flight of the Buffalo* to many of her clients.

Terri is best known as "Mom" to two young men and "Wife" to Les Wiest. They live near Branson, Missouri, on Table Rock Lake.

www.ingramcontent.com/pod-product-compliance
Lightning Source LLC
Chambersburg PA
CBHW071359210526
45465CB00001B/167